OPPOSING
VIEWPOINTS®
SERIES

Social Justice

Other Books of Related Interest:

Opposing Viewpoints Series

American Values

Civil Liberties

Male and Female Roles

At Issue Series

Affirmative Action

Is Racism a Serious Problem?

Current Controversies Series

Racism

The Wage Gap

"Congress shall make no law . . . abridging the freedom of speech, or of the press."

First Amendment to the U.S. Constitution

The basic foundation of our democracy is the First Amendment guarantee of freedom of expression. The *Opposing Viewpoints* series is dedicated to the concept of this basic freedom and the idea that it is more important to practice it than to enshrine it.

Social Justice

David Haugen, Susan Musser, and Vickey Kalambakal,
Book Editors

GREENHAVEN PRESS
A part of Gale, Cengage Learning

GALE
CENGAGE Learning™

Detroit • New York • San Francisco • New Haven, Conn • Waterville, Maine • London

Christine Nasso, *Publisher*
Elizabeth Des Chenes, *Managing Editor*

For more information, contact:
Greenhaven Press
27500 Drake Rd.
Farmington Hills, MI 48331-3535
Or you can visit our Internet site at gale.cengage.com

For product information and technology assistance, contact us at

Gale Customer Support, 1-800-877-4253
For permission to use material from this text or product, submit all requests online at www.cengage.com/permissions

Further permissions questions can be emailed to permissionrequest@cengage.com

Articles in Greenhaven Press anthologies are often edited for length to meet page requirements. In addition, original titles of these works are changed to clearly present the main thesis and to explicitly indicate the author's opinion. Every effort is made to ensure that Greenhaven Press accurately reflects the original intent of the authors. Every effort has been made to trace the owners of copyrighted material.

Image copyright Lucian Coman, 2010. Used under license from Shutterstock.com.

LIBRARY OF CONGRESS CATALOGING-IN-PUBLICATION DATA

Social justice / David Haugen, Susan Musser, and Vickey Kalambakal, book editors.
    p. cm. -- (Opposing viewpoints)
    Includes bibliographical references and index.
    ISBN 978-0-7377-4783-6 (hardcover) -- ISBN 978-0-7377-4784-3 (pbk.)
    1. Social justice--United States. I. Haugen, David M., 1969- II. Musser, Susan. III. Kalambakal, Vickey.
    HM671.S623 2010
    303.3'72--dc22
                                        2009050450

Printed in the United States of America
1 2 3 4 5 6 7 14 13 12 11 10

Contents

Chapter 3: What Policies Would Promote Social Justice for Women?

Chapter 4: What Global Policies Promote Social Justice?

Why Consider Opposing Viewpoints?

> "The only way in which a human being can make some approach to knowing the whole of a subject is by hearing what can be said about it by persons of every variety of opinion and studying all modes in which it can be looked at by every character of mind. No wise man ever acquired his wisdom in any mode but this."
>
> John Stuart Mill

In our media-intensive culture it is not difficult to find differing opinions. Thousands of newspapers and magazines and dozens of radio and television talk shows resound with differing points of view. The difficulty lies in deciding which opinion to agree with and which "experts" seem the most credible. The more inundated we become with differing opinions and claims, the more essential it is to hone critical reading and thinking skills to evaluate these ideas. Opposing Viewpoints books address this problem directly by presenting stimulating debates that can be used to enhance and teach these skills. The varied opinions contained in each book examine many different aspects of a single issue. While examining these conveniently edited opposing views, readers can develop critical thinking skills such as the ability to compare and contrast authors' credibility, facts, argumentation styles, use of persuasive techniques, and other stylistic tools. In short, the Opposing Viewpoints Series is an ideal way to attain the higher-level thinking and reading skills so essential in a culture of diverse and contradictory opinions.

In addition to providing a tool for critical thinking, *Opposing Viewpoints* books challenge readers to question their own strongly held opinions and assumptions. Most people form their opinions on the basis of upbringing, peer pressure, and personal, cultural, or professional bias. By reading carefully balanced opposing views, readers must directly confront new ideas as well as the opinions of those with whom they disagree. This is not to simplistically argue that everyone who reads opposing views will—or should—change his or her opinion. Instead, the series enhances readers' understanding of their own views by encouraging confrontation with opposing ideas. Careful examination of others' views can lead to the readers' understanding of the logical inconsistencies in their own opinions, perspective on why they hold an opinion, and the consideration of the possibility that their opinion requires further evaluation.

Evaluating Other Opinions

To ensure that this type of examination occurs, *Opposing Viewpoints* books present all types of opinions. Prominent spokespeople on different sides of each issue as well as well-known professionals from many disciplines challenge the reader. An additional goal of the series is to provide a forum for other, less known, or even unpopular viewpoints. The opinion of an ordinary person who has had to make the decision to cut off life support from a terminally ill relative, for example, may be just as valuable and provide just as much insight as a medical ethicist's professional opinion. The editors have two additional purposes in including these less known views. One, the editors encourage readers to respect others' opinions—even when not enhanced by professional credibility. It is only by reading or listening to and objectively evaluating others' ideas that one can determine whether they are worthy of consideration. Two, the inclusion of such viewpoints encourages the important critical thinking skill of objectively evaluating an author's credentials and bias. This evaluation will illuminate an author's reasons for taking a particular stance on an issue and will aid in readers' evaluation of the author's ideas.

It is our hope that these books will give readers a deeper understanding of the issues debated and an appreciation of the complexity of even seemingly simple issues when good and honest people disagree. This awareness is particularly important in a democratic society such as ours in which people enter into public debate to determine the common good. Those with whom one disagrees should not be regarded as enemies but rather as people whose views deserve careful examination and may shed light on one's own.

Thomas Jefferson once said that "difference of opinion leads to inquiry, and inquiry to truth." Jefferson, a broadly educated man, argued that "if a nation expects to be ignorant and free . . . it expects what never was and never will be." As individuals and as a nation, it is imperative that we consider the opinions of others and examine them with skill and discernment. The *Opposing Viewpoints* series is intended to help readers achieve this goal.

David L. Bender and Bruno Leone,
Founders

Introduction

> "For us the primary subject of justice is the basic structure of society, or more exactly, the way in which the major social institutions distribute fundamental rights and duties and determine the division of advantages from social cooperation. By major institutions I understand the political constitution and the principal economic and social arrangements."
>
> John Rawls,
> A Theory of Justice, 1971.

Social justice is a rather indistinct term that can mean different things to different people. Commonly, social justice is a policy-making theory that tries to ensure that all members of society are treated fairly and that all have the same opportunities to partake of and share in the benefits of society. For some, this may mean an end to discrimination based on race, creed, ethnicity, income, or sex. Others might favor economic justice that seeks to provide equality through fair taxation and the distribution of wealth, resources, and property. Still others might insist that social justice promotes equal access to education and job placement. Many social justice advocates believe that the term can encompass all this and more.

Often the concept of social justice arises not as a forward-thinking measure brought up in Utopian visions of the world as it could be, but as a defensive stance that rallies critics of current disparities that plague a global society seemingly divided into haves and have-nots. For example, various pro-environment, pro-equality political organizations that band together under the name of the Green Party base their activism on a credo known as the Four Pillars, one of which is the pursuit of social justice. The American Green Party states, "We must consciously confront in ourselves, our organizations, and society at large, barriers such as racism and class oppression, sexism and homophobia, ageism and disability, which act to deny fair treatment and equal justice under the law," while the Irish Green Party avers that it is against "control of industry by large national and multinational companies" as well as "the exploitation of the third world." Thus, these organizations view social justice as a policy worth following if present-day society is to be more equitable.

The social justice program hinges on the assumption that the disparity between rich and poor, the advantaged and disadvantaged, needs to be rectified or overcome if a truly just society (whether global, national, or local) is to emerge. Most proponents of social justice point to the unequal distribution of wealth when arguing their case. For example, according to research done in 2007 by New York University economist Edward N. Wolff, the richest 1 percent of the U.S. population owned 34.3 percent of the nation's privately held wealth (stocks, bonds, property, and other marketable assets), while the top 10 percent held 71 percent. At the other extreme, the poorest 40 percent owned a mere 1 percent of the nation's wealth, according to Wolff. In comparison, a study by the World Institute for Development Economics Research concluded that the top 10 percent of the world's population held 85 percent of global wealth (including all assets). University of California psychology and sociology professor G. William Domhoff explains that the gap between the richest and poorest has been growing over time—chiefly due to tax breaks and the decline of organized labor. Domhoff also contends that with wealth comes power, power to maintain the status quo so that the concentration of wealth will remain in the hands of the few.

Looking beyond financial wealth, however, social justice advocates insist that a global disparity exists between those who do and do not have access to natural resources as well as those who do and do not share the benefits of education and technological innovation. The Environmental News Service claims that 880 million people worldwide do not have access to clean drinking water, and in March 2009, the agency reported that twenty countries banded together to protest the World Water Forum's classification of water as a human need not a human right. In the words of United Nations General Assembly president Miguel D'Escoto, "Water is a public trust, a common heritage of people and nature, and a fundamental human right. . . . We must challenge the notion that water is a commodity to be bought and sold on the open market. Those who are committed to the privatization of water . . . are denying people a human right as basic as the air we breathe." Such protests exemplify the confrontations that arise when governments debate the unequal distribution of resources such as water, food, oil, and wood. These debates are intensified by the fact that most natural resources are held by industrialized nations in the Northern Hemisphere, while those developing countries in Sub-Saharan Africa and other parts of the Third World are lacking. Thus, the divide between haves and have-nots often gets framed as a divide between the developed North and the impoverished, disadvantaged South.

Despite the fact that global resources are not equally spread across the planet and the fact that an elite few hold a high percentage of the world's wealth, not everyone endorses the "have and have-not" division or sees it as problematic. According to a 2007 Pew Research poll, Americans, for example, were divided on the issue of class division. Roughly 48 percent of those polled agreed that the nation was split between haves and have-nots, and about 48 percent disagreed with this assessment. Still, the number of dissenters was quite higher (71 percent) only a decade ago in 1988. In addition, most critics of an economic justice strategy that seeks to spread the wealth among rich and poor alike contend that it would be punitive to those who worked hard to make their fortunes. Condemning President Barack Obama's campaign remark about intending to "spread the wealth" in America, radio personality and political pundit Lowell Ponte stated, "This can only be done by first expropriating, i.e., stealing, what others have earned; in effect, stealing a large part of their life, energy, and talent and robbing opportunities from their children." Often critics of this vein further their arguments by claiming that the only people who will benefit from spreading the wealth are those who do not work hard and are willing to sponge off others. In fact a popular bumper sticker and T-shirt slogan attests "Don't Spread My Wealth, Spread My Work Ethic."

Extending this argument to a global perspective, some opponents of "international welfare" advocate that work and trade are still the keys to bettering the lot of the world's poor—especially if these assets are not fettered by protectionist policies or undemocratic governments. For example, many free trade proponents believe that economic opportunities, prosperity, and even equitable justice within poor countries will come with globalization, the opening of markets and the integrating of trade around the world. Tom G. Palmer, a senior fellow at the libertarian Cato Institute, states, "Within countries that have opened their economies to trade and investment, middle classes have grown, which means less income inequality." Palmer also stipulates that opening markets in developing nations also tends to reduce child labor and brings about better governments, which in turn promotes justice through the rule of law. Palmer even claims that "free trade is not a privilege; it is a human right," reinforcing the notion that social justice on a global scale would be improved if this "right" were respected.

Whether social justice will require the redistribution of wealth, resources, and advantages is still a hotly debated argument. In *Opposing Viewpoints: Social Justice*, politicians, experts, and social critics proffer different strategies for bringing about a more just society both in the United States and around the globe. In chapters that ask Should America Do More to Reduce Economic Inequality? What Policies Would Promote Social Justice for Minorities? What Policies Would Promote Social Justice for Women? and What Global Policies Promote Social Justice? some of the commentators and policy makers develop theories on how to achieve social justice, while others question the necessity or cost of putting these ideas into practice. All wish to see a more just society, but not everyone agrees on the path to achieving that justice. Finding the right path—or paths—may bring society closer to equality under the law and in the marketplace. Taking the wrong course may lead to class warfare or exacerbate gender, ethnic, or racial divisions for decades to come.

CHAPTER 1

Should America Do More to Reduce Economic Inequality?

Chapter Preface

By 2007, the richest 10 percent of families in the United States acquired nearly half of all income in the country. This percentage of income—49.74, to be exact—is the highest ever recorded. To see such a huge chunk of U.S. income going to one-tenth of U.S. families is atypical; in fact, the last time that such a small fraction held over 49 percent of income was in 1928, nearly eighty years before today's peak. As a comparison, between 1945 and 1980 an average of 34 percent of income went to the top tenth of U.S. households.

When that top decile, or tenth, is broken down further, economists find that the bulk of income is really going to only 1 percent of U.S. households. Professor Emmanuel Saez of the University of California at Berkeley tracks the income gap between rich and poor, and his figures show that 1 percent of U.S. families now collect 23.5 percent of the nation's income. Much of the wealth comes from large stock portfolios and capital gains. The average income of the top 1 percent is over a million dollars a year. Put another way, the three hundred thousand people in the top tier earned, on average, 440 times as much as the average family in the bottom half—where 150 million of the total 305 million Americans find themselves.

That 1 per cent of the population holds so much of the country's income alarms many economists, social scientists, politicians, and commentators. They worry that the rich are getting richer while the poor grow poorer, a saying that became popular during the U.S. Great Depression of the 1930s. "When income growth is concentrated at the top of the income scale, the people at the bottom have a much harder time lifting themselves out of poverty and giving their children a decent start in life," states Jared Bernstein, a progressive economist and advisor in the administration of President Barack Obama.

Republican columnist David Frum accuses fellow conservatives of simply ignoring the income gap and "being not bothered by the accumulation of wealth as such." But he warns, "Inequality taken to extremes can overwhelm conservative ideals of self-reliance, limited government and national unity. It can delegitimize commerce and business and invite destructive protectionism and overregulation. Inequality, in short, is a conservative issue too."

Frum does not speak for all conservatives, however. Talk show host Michael Medved believes that the income gap is not as one-sided as it appears. Medved reports in a 2009 Town hall.com article, "As the rich get richer, the poor also get richer, dramatically richer—but redistributionists [those who want to spread the wealth among all classes] express horror at the fact that the distance between the least and most successful continues to increase." In short, he believes the gap is widening but the greatest gain in wealth is being made by the nation's poor. "Far from being left behind," Medved attests, "the least privileged Americans are making faster progress than any other segment of the population."

The viewpoints in the following chapter describe differing views on the challenges of economic inequality. The authors examine popular solutions that have been proposed over the years and express their opinions on whether these solutions would correct the disparity in American incomes or create new problems.

"Our class is able to do battle, through the unions for example. To that extent, we can win a greater share of the surplus value."

Workers Must Fight to Close the Income Gap

Oriando Ibarra

In the following viewpoint, Oriando Ibarra, a student at the City University of New York, argues that there is an income gap in America between the owning class and the working class. As Ibarra claims, chief executives make more than four hundred times the income of workers, and increased efforts on the part of workers generally raise the profits of owners but does not typically benefit the wages of the proletariat, or working class. Noting the vibrant history of class struggle in America, Ibarra asserts that workers will make gains in the marketplace only if they continue to struggle against the class system.

As you read, consider the following questions:

1. As Ibarra defines it, what is surplus value?

2. In the author's estimation, what happened to the U.S. gross domestic product between 1970 and 2003?

Oriando Ibarra, "Class Struggle and the Widening Income Gap," *Socialism & Liberation*, vol. 3, November 2006. Reproduced by permission.

3. What blame does Ibarra attach to news reporters who covered the "enormous shift in wealth" over the past several years?

An Aug. 28 [2006] article in the *New York Times* highlighted the reality of the U.S. capitalist economy today. Titled "Real wages fail to match a rise in productivity," journalists Steven Greenhouse and David Leonhardt point to the fact that despite huge increases in the productivity and profit of the capitalist economy as a whole, workers have not seen comparable benefits.

"With the economy beginning to slow," Greenhouse and Leonhardt write, "the current expansion has a chance to become the first sustained period of economic growth since World War II that fails to offer a prolonged increase in real wages for most workers."

The article points to new statistics from the [U.S.] Labor Department showing that "worker productivity rose 16.6 percent from 2000 to 2005, while total compensation for the median worker rose 7.2 percent in the same five year period. . . ."

Exploiting the Workers

Wealth is being extracted from U.S. workers at a higher and higher rate. The statistics reported in the *Times* illustrate the point graphically—although the article does not call it by its name: exploitation. It is the extraction of surplus value from workers to owners, from the proletariat to the bourgeoisie, from producers to profiteers.

And it is what socialists have been talking about since the times of [socialism's originator, philosopher] Karl Marx. In his 1847 pamphlet, "Wage-Labor and Capital," Marx explained that what is good for the boss is bad for the worker. "The interests of capital and the interests of wage-labor are diametrically opposed to each other," he wrote. "Profit and wages remain as before, in inverse proportion."

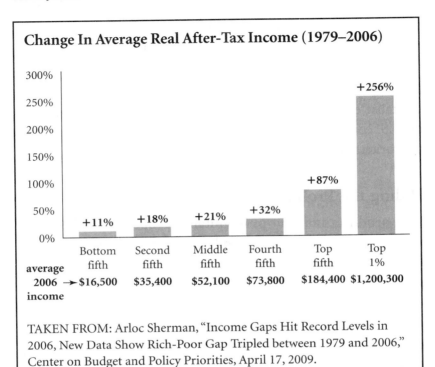

Change In Average Real After-Tax Income (1979–2006)

	Bottom fifth	Second fifth	Middle fifth	Fourth fifth	Top fifth	Top 1%
change	+11%	+18%	+21%	+32%	+87%	+256%
average 2006 income	$16,500	$35,400	$52,100	$73,800	$184,400	$1,200,300

TAKEN FROM: Arloc Sherman, "Income Gaps Hit Record Levels in 2006, New Data Show Rich-Poor Gap Tripled between 1979 and 2006," Center on Budget and Policy Priorities, April 17, 2009.

More than that: Brooks claims that now it is the right people getting the wealth! Paraphrasing Clinton administration official Lawrence Katz, he claims, "The market increasingly rewards people with high social and customer-service skills."

"In other words," Brooks asserts, "the market is not broken; the meritocracy is working almost too well."

Workers Must Engage in Class Struggle

Right-wing propaganda aside, the Aug. 28 *Times* article does point to a real source of the growing wealth gap: the attacks on the labor movement. They quote Goldman Sachs economists saying, "The most important contributor to higher profit margins over the past five years has been a decline in labor's share of national income."

Jared Bernstein from the Economic Policy Institute is more blunt: "[I]t comes down to bargaining power and the lack of ability of many in the work force to claim their fair share of growth."

In other words, the decades-old war on the U.S. labor movement is showing up on the accountants' ledgers. It is the class struggle—in this case, the ruling class's attacks on working people to drive down wages and drive up profits.

But this also shows the way to reversing this trend. The United States has a rich history of working class struggle— although we are denied that knowledge at every step of our education, from kindergarten to college. Every one of the reforms we enjoy today, even though they are inadequate, was won in struggle.

Our class is able to do battle, through the unions for example. To that extent, we can win a greater share of the surplus value.

As socialists and communists, we do not have a perspective of doom and gloom. Rather, it is one of responsibility and action. It is up to us to find the way forward. Those of us in the unions need to be working to "fight to make our unions fight."

But we know that this trend will not be turned around in shop-by-shop battles. That is where a national party like ours can have an impact, trying to intervene not just with local fights but on a national and international scale on a class-conscious basis.

So lock and load, my brothers and sisters, and I will see you on the battlefield—the battlefield of the class struggle.

| "When you look at the really big picture, it's apparent that living standards are rising across the entire spectrum of incomes."

The Income Gap
Is Exaggerated

Brad Schiller

Brad Schiller is a professor of economics at American University in Washington, D.C. and at the University of Nevada–Reno. In the viewpoint that follows, Schiller contends that the income gap in America is not an indication that the rich are getting richer and the poor are getting poorer. Instead, Schiller claims incomes have consistently risen in recent decades for all economic groups. This, he argues, is borne out by the fact that more Americans of all stripes are indulging in luxury goods and purchasing new homes and cars. Schiller refutes the notion of a drastically widening income gap by indicating that measurements of household income do not typically track families and individuals as they climb up the class ladder, nor do they account for demographic changes in America that include a growing immigrant population.

As you read, consider the following questions:

1. According to Schiller, by what percent has the average income of the poorest Americans risen between 1970 and 2006?

2. How has the composition of "typical" households changed since 1970, as Schiller reports?

3. How does the author use the "March Madness" ticket-line analogy to explain the changing character of lower- and middle-class income distribution?

Class warfare is once again a campaign theme [in 2008]. The Democratic candidates are railing against the "tax cuts for the rich," lamenting the stagnation of middle-class incomes, and decrying the deepening woes of the poor. In her January response to President [George W.] Bush's State of the Union address, [presidential candidate New York senator] Hillary Clinton cited "seven years of stagnant wages, declining incomes and increasing inequality." [Presidential candidate Illinois senator] Barack Obama echoes this theme by referring repeatedly to the "middle-class squeeze."

Both candidates portray America as a nation where the fruits of economic progress have been usurped by corporate CEOs [chief executive officers], equity-fund managers, inside traders and international speculators. Main Street has floundered, while Wall Street has flourished.

Popular Misconceptions

The annual release of census data on household incomes provides the foundation for the "two Americas" thesis. The latest figures tracked changes in incomes all the way back to 1967. Two observations grabbed the headlines. First, the data indicate that the top-earning 20% of households get half of all the income generated in the country, while the lowest-earning 20% of households get a meager 3.4%. That disparity has widened over time: In 1970, their respective shares were 43.3% and 4.1%. These income-share numbers buttress the popular notion that the "rich are getting richer while the poor are getting poorer."

The second observation in the Census reports relates to the well-being of the middle class. The median household income in 2006 was $48,201, just a trifle ahead of its 1998 level ($48,034). That seems to confirm middle-class stagnation.

While there is some substance to these fears of widening inequality and middle-class stagnation, the situation is not nearly as clear-cut. Demographic changes in the size and composition of U.S. households have distorted the statistics in important ways.

Economic Growth Across the Board

First, we can easily dismiss the notion that the poor are getting poorer. All the Census Bureau tells us is that the share of the pie consumed by the poor has been shrinking (to 3.4% in 2006 from 4.1% in 1970). But the "pie" has grown enormously. This year's [2008's] real GDP [gross domestic product] of $14 trillion is three times that of 1970. So the absolute size of the slice received by the bottom 20% has increased to $476 billion from $181 billion. Allowing for population growth shows that the average income of people at the bottom of the income distribution has risen 36%.

They're not rich, but they're certainly not poorer. In reality, economic growth has raised incomes across the board.

The Census data originate from an annual survey of households. The data don't track individual households from year to year, but instead just take a snapshot of the households in existence in March of each year. From these annual snapshots, we try to infer what's happening to the typical household over time.

The "typical" household, however, keeps changing. Since 1970 there has been a dramatic rise in divorced, never-married

Income Gap Is Necessary

In a free society, there will be and *should* be differences in income. That's because some people are better at serving consumers than others—more innovative, more ambitious, more energetic, more intelligent. Why should they be denied their just rewards for making our lives better? And whom would we hurt most if we deny them? Mainly ourselves.

Sheldon Richman, Future of Freedom Foundation, June 2005.

and single-person households. Back in 1970, the married Ozzie and Harriet family [referring to a 1950s TV family of married parents and two children] was the norm: 71% of all U.S. households were two-parent families. Now the ratio is only 51%. In the process of this social revolution, the average household size has shrunk to 2.57 persons from 3.14—a drop of 18%. The meaning? Even a "stagnant" average household income implies a higher standard of living for the average household member.

A More Realistic Snapshot

Last year [2007], the Census Bureau published a new set of income statistics that adjusted for changing household size and composition. In a single year (2006), this "equivalence-adjusted" computation increased the income share of the poor by 8% and reduced the standard measure of inequality (Gini coefficient) by 4%. Such "equivalency" adjustments would mute unadjusted inequality trends even more.

A closer look at household trends reveals that the percentage of one-person households has jumped to 27% from 17%. That's right: More than one out of four U.S. households now has only one occupant. Who are these people? Overwhelmingly, they are Generation Xers whose good jobs and high pay have permitted them to move out of their parental homes and establish their own residences. The rest are largely seniors who have enough savings and income to escape from their grandchildren and enjoy the serenity of an independent household. Both transitions are evidence of rising affluence, not increasing hardship. Yet this splintering of the extended family exerts strong downward statistical pressure on the average income of U.S. households. Had the Generation Xers and their affluent grandparents all stayed under the same roof the average household income would be higher, but most of us would be worse off.

The supposed decline of the poor and middle class is exaggerated even more by the dynamics of population growth. When people look at the "poor" in any two years, they think they're looking at the same people. That's rarely true, especially over longer periods of time.

Since 1998, the U.S. population has increased by over 20 million. Nearly half of that growth has come from immigration, legal and illegal. Overwhelmingly, these immigrants enter at the lowest rungs on the income ladder. Statistically, this immigrant surge not only reduces the income of the "average" household, but also changes the occupants of the lowest income classes.

To understand what's happening here, envision a line of people queued up for March Madness [men's college basketball tournament] tickets. Individuals move up the line as tickets are purchased. But new people keep coming. So the line never gets shorter, even though individuals are advancing.

Something similar happens with the distribution of income. People keep entering the distribution line from the bottom. Even though individuals are moving up the line, the middle of the line never seems to move. Hence, an unchanged—or even receding—median marker could co-exist with individual advancement. The people who were at the middle marker before have moved up the distribution line. This is the kind of income mobility that has long characterized U.S. income dynamics.

All Incomes Are Rising

When you look at the really big picture, it's apparent that living standards are rising across the entire spectrum of incomes. Just since 2000, GDP has risen by 18% while the population has grown by 6%. So per capita incomes have clearly been rising. The growth of per capita income since 1980 or 1970 has simply been spectacular. Some people would have you believe that all of this added income was funneled to the rich. But the math doesn't work out.

The increase in nominal GDP since 2000 amounts to over $4 trillion annually. If you assume that all that money went to the wealthiest 10% of U.S. households, that bonanza would come to a whopping $350,000 per household. Yet according to the Census Bureau, the top 10% of households has an average income of $200,000 or so. The implied bonanza is so absurd that the notion that only the rich have gained from the economic growth can be dismissed out of hand. Clearly, there is a lot of economic advancement across a broad swath of population. Dramatic changes in household composition, household size and immigration tend to obscure this reality.

That broad swath of economic advancement shows up in personal consumption. According to the Labor Department, personal consumption spending has risen by $2.5 trillion since 2000. More Americans own homes and new cars today than ever before, despite slowdowns in both industries. Laptop computers, iPhones and flat-panel TVs are fast becoming necessities rather than luxury items.

The average American household is doing pretty well. The evident gap between income realities and political rhetoric may help explain why the "two Americas" theme, first asserted by [Democratic nominee for president in 2004 and 2008] John Edwards and since echoed by Mrs. Clinton and Mr. Obama, may ultimately fail to resonate with voters. On Election Day, voters may well turn to the candidate with the greater focus on a strong economy that increases everyone's income.

"It's time we had a [tax] system through which people didn't have to figure out ways to cheat in order to save their money."

America Needs the Fair Tax System

Chuck Norris

In the following viewpoint, veteran action film and television actor Chuck Norris argues that the United States should dispense with income taxes and support the Fair Tax system that would tax only imports and consumer goods. Norris believes that the Fair Tax system is what the Founding Fathers envisioned to provide revenue for the government. He maintains that the Constitution specifically outlaws income taxes and export taxes because the Founding Fathers did not want to discourage productivity and innovation.

As you read, consider the following questions:

1. What are some of the elements of the "maze of taxes" that Norris says Americans have to navigate today?

2. As the author explains, why was the IRS established?

3. Why would a Fair Tax system be the "world's biggest economic jumper cables," according to the FairTax Web site as cited by Norris?

Teatime, anyone? I hope you've joined one of the thousands of TEA (Taxed Enough Already) parties or FairTax rallies, which are happening across the country April 15 [2009] to protest outrageous government spending, the deepening of our national debt, and the subsequent taxes. This is a nonpartisan time to rally around like-minded citizens and declare that we're tired of the same old political rhetoric and that we want a better way.

I personally encourage all people to voice to their representatives that we need to return to a taxation system similar to the one established by our Founding Fathers. They did not penalize productivity through taxes the way we do today. They had no Internal Revenue Service [IRS]. They believed in minimal taxation. They did *not* pay income taxes, which were prohibited by the Constitution. They did *not* pay export taxes, which also were prohibited by the Constitution. But they did tax imports. The Founders believed in free trade within our own borders and a system of tariffs on imported goods.

Keeping Taxation Simple

That's a system that makes sense to me. It is a system designed to preserve individual liberty and encourage productivity (through no income taxes and no discouragement of domestic production through export taxes) while choosing to keep taxes as painless as possible (through taxes on foreign imports). And it doesn't require an IRS to run it.

The Founders would have been horrified at the bloated federal bureaucracy we have now and the maze of taxes we have to navigate: income taxes, employment taxes, capital gains taxes, estate taxes, corporate taxes, property taxes, Social Security taxes, gas taxes, etc. It was excessive taxation like this that drove the Founders to rebel in the first place.

All of the Founders were opposed to domestic taxes. They regarded high taxes and aggressive tax collectors as tyrannical and always to be guarded against. Patrick Henry warned: "Excisemen may come in multitudes, for the limitation of their numbers no man knows. They may, unless the general government be restrained by a bill of rights or some similar restriction, go into your cellars and rooms and search, ransack and measure everything you eat, drink and wear." (A prophetic statement?)

The IRS wasn't started until nearly 100 years after the Revolutionary War, in 1862 as the Bureau of Internal Revenue. Its creation coincided with the creation of the income tax, which it was designed to collect. Both were the work of President Abraham Lincoln and Congress, who saw them as necessary to pay for Civil War expenses.

It is interesting to note, however, that the income tax law 10 years later, was revived in 1894, and then was ruled by the Supreme Court as unconstitutional in 1895. Yet in 1913, it became law through the 16th Amendment. Ever since then, the income tax has deprived families of their rightful earnings, restricted our liberties, and deprived our economy of money that could have been invested in productive enterprises.

Abolish the IRS

Today the IRS is the No. 1 enemy of your pocketbook. Who doesn't fear an IRS audit? It's the only federal agency that considers you guilty until proven innocent. It can't be overhauled or even reformed (Congress' attempts have failed).

The best answer is to abolish the IRS, sweep away the present tax code, and implement FairTax's plan, which lives up to its name. As [former governor of Arkansas and Republican presidential candidate] Mike Huckabee says, "Wouldn't it be nice if April 15 were just another sunny spring day?"

FairTax's plan would do away with all taxes and would put in their place a single consumptive (fair) tax, which right now

The FairTax System

New economic research shows that the economy fares much better under the FairTax. The economy as measured by GDP [gross domestic product] is 2.4 percent higher in the first year [after implementation of the Fair-Tax plan] and 11.3 percent higher by the tenth year than it would otherwise be. Consumption increases by 2.4 percent more in the first year than it would be if the current system were to remain in place. The increase in consumption is fueled by the 1.7 percent increase in disposable (after tax) personal income that accompanies the rise in incomes from capital and labor once the FairTax is enacted. By the tenth year consumption increases by 11.7 percent over what it would be if the current tax system remained in place, and disposable income will be up by 11.8 percent.

Following the implementation of the FairTax plan, the higher take-home wage provides an immediate incentive for people to work more. During the first year, this will lead to total employment growth of 3.5 percent in excess of the baseline scenario, which continues to grow through year ten such that total employment is 9.0 percent above what it would have been under the baseline scenario.

Americans for Fair Taxation,
"The FairTax: Fundamentals and Facts," 2007.
www.fairtax.org.

is the closest practical proposal to the taxation system favored by the Founders [of the United States]. With the fair tax, the harder you worked and the more money you made the better off you and our economy would be. You would pay taxes only when you bought something, which means that you could control how much you'd be taxed and that you never would be penalized for working hard.

It's time we had a system through which people didn't have to figure out ways to cheat in order to save their money. Again, as Huckabee says: "The fair tax is a completely transparent tax system. It doesn't increase taxes. It's revenue-neutral. But here's what it will do: It will bring business back to the United States that is leaving our shores because our tax laws make it impossible for an American-based business to compete. . . . The fair tax was designed by economists from Harvard and Stanford and some of the leading think tanks across the country."

Restore the Nation's Economy

There are also trillions of dollars hiding in offshore accounts. With the fair tax, the people with their money offshore could bring it back to invest here, which would give a huge boost to our economy. It's the biggest stimulation package there is. As the FairTax Web site says, "Think of it as the World's Biggest Economic Jumper Cables."

If the Founding Fathers were here today, I believe they would support the fair tax. As James Madison said, "Taxes on consumption are always least burdensome because they are least felt and are borne, too, by those who are both willing and able to pay them; that of all taxes on consumption, those on foreign commerce are most compatible with the genius and policy of free states."

We don't need more tax reform. We need a tax revolution! And FairTax's plan would provide it. If we all jumped on the bandwagon and demanded our representatives implement such a taxation system, we could restore our nation economically and make the financially impossible become possible again.

> "[Proponents] argue that the advantage
> of "Fair Tax" is that . . . it applies
> equally and fairly to all across the
> board. All of these arguments are falla-
> cious."

The Fair Tax System Is Unfair

Steve Crawley

Steve Crawley is an emeritus professor and the former director of the Criminal Justice Department at Virginia College in Huntsville, Alabama. He is now engaged in consulting, traveling, writing, and politics. In the following viewpoint, Crawley contends that the Fair Tax system is deceptive and untenable. As Crawley states, the Fair Tax rate (a tax on consumption) would have to be quite high to cover the money needed to fill government budgets. In addition, Crawley notes that the finances required to administer and police the new system would likely drive the Fair Tax rate even higher—perhaps more than 10 percent higher than the current income tax rate. In Crawley's view, few Americans would consent to such staggering taxation.

As you read, consider the following questions:

1. In Crawley's opinion, why is the 23 percent Fair Tax taxation rate deceptive?

Steve Crawley, "'Fair Tax' Is Unfair," e-wisdom, June 7, 2009. Reproduced by permission of the author.

2. What are some of the hidden costs that Crawley says are often overlooked in carrying out the Fair Tax rebate program?

3. According to the author, what sales taxation rate did the Treasury Department figure would be necessary to replace the income tax system in 2005?

The day after the "Fair Tax" goes into effect, I will have enough money in my savings account to purchase that 2008 Ford Truck that I have been saving for. I paid income tax on the saved money as I earned it, and now I must pay the "Fair Tax" again when I buy the truck. A friend of mine also bought a truck the day before the "Fair Tax" started. He borrowed the money and purchased a 2008 Ford Truck just like mine. He did not pay income tax on the money when he borrowed it, nor did he pay the "Fair Tax" when he used it to buy the truck.

Now, we both own similar trucks purchased a day apart—yet I paid federal taxes twice on the same money, but my friend paid no federal taxes at all. Under any value system, moral code, or just plain common sense, this situation has to be "unfair" and "unjust." To make matter worse, my friend's debt payments for the truck are specifically exempted from the "Fair Tax."

This same scenario would play out for buying a house or any other major purchase. It would also be true for all routine living expenses if the money being spent comes from savings. Considering the huge dollar volume of savings in this country, this would result in a massive wealth transfer from people who are savers to people who borrow. It makes no economic sense to punish the thrifty to reward the spendthrift. If anything, savers should be rewarded.

Hiding the True Costs

In response, "Fair Tax" advocates argue that the profits from tax-deferred [investments] escape income tax if profits are taken after the "Fair Tax" starts. However, this is not a benefit because profit from untaxed invested savings after the "Fair Tax" is not taxed anyway. This rule is also deceptively touted as equal to the debtor's benefit of a tax exemption. They also argue that the advantage of "Fair Tax" is that it drives out the hidden taxes of the old system, and that it applies equally and fairly to all across the board. All of these arguments are fallacious.

The true "Fair Tax" rate is camouflaged. People naturally equate the advocated 23% national sales tax to the state sales taxes they are familiar with. A state 5% sales tax means that one pays $1.05 at the checkout for an item priced at $1. Therefore, they assume that under the "Fair Tax," they would pay $1.23 for an item priced at $1.

In fact, the rate is not 23%, but 30%. The 23% rate is arrived at by treating the tax as if it were already part of the price instead of being on top. Thus, if a product were to sell for $1 and the "Fair Tax" added 30%, the 30-cent tax comes to 23% of $1.30. This is how a 30% rate is deceptively turned into a 23% rate.

It is obvious why this subterfuge is maintained. Polls show that support for flat-rate tax schemes falls sharply at a rate higher than 23%. Furthermore, the vast majority of taxpayers pay less than 23% in federal income taxes now, so support for the "Fair Tax" would likely evaporate if people generally understood that the rate is 30% instead of 23%.

Governments must also pay the "Fair Tax." In order to make it seem as if a 23% rate is high enough to equal current federal revenues, the "Fair Tax" is applied to all government purchases at every level. Only education spending is exempted. In addition to the massive federal spending increase needed to pay the 30% "Fair Tax," states will have to pay 30% more on every highway and bridge they build, local governments will have to pay 30% more for police and fire protection, and even the federal government will have to pay the tax to itself when

Everyone Is a Tax Collector

Although the FairTax would eliminate the filing of all individual tax returns, the FairTax turns every business into a tax collector. Every small service business and every Internet business that does not currently collect state sales taxes will have to collect taxes for the federal government. Every doctor will now have to charge sales tax on his services. Where will this end? Will the neighborhood boy who mows lawns have to begin collecting federal sales tax on each lawn mowed? Will the neighborhood girl who baby sits have to do likewise?

Laurence M. Vance, Mises Daily,
May 18, 2005. http://mises.org

it buys weapons and ammunition for our troops. Taxes will have to increase at all governmental levels to pay for the additional 30% government spending. However, "Fair Tax" supporters dishonestly exclude this higher spending from their calculations.

De Facto National Welfare

The "Fair Tax" rebate program[1] adds $600 billion to federal spending annually. "Fair Tax" supporters say the rebate is just like what we get back when tax withholding exceeds our taxes. In fact, it is more like Social Security because it comes in a monthly check instead of at the end of the year. Aside from the incredible complexity and intrusiveness of tracking every

1. Under the FairTax plan, households would receive a rebate every month to return to individuals and families part of the money spent on necessities such as food, clothing, and shelter. The amount of the rebate for each household depends on household income—the higher the income, the smaller the rebate.

American's monthly income—and creating a de facto national welfare program—the "Fair Tax" does not include the cost of this rebate in the tax rate.

Costs of monthly inventorying family size, and administratively managing the check mailings and postage costs each month to execute the rebate program are also not covered in the "Fair Tax." Attempts to diffuse it throughout the states by mandate cannot work because the costs will still be there. There will be administrative costs for policing all the purveyors of goods and services for compliance, "used" versus "new" compliance, black marketing, bartering, etc. The current IRS [Internal Revenue Service] multi-billion budgets, which are alleged to go away once the "Fair Tax" is implemented, will not be enough.

Over time, enforcement measures will become more draconian [harsh] than they are today: especially since a massive retail sales tax would create a massive incentive to evade it. What's to stop people from bypassing retail outlets and buying their goods from producers or at wholesale, tax-free? That's why every country that has ever tried to impose retail sales taxes this high has quickly moved to a Value Added Tax levied at every stage of production. Consumers rarely see or keep track of these taxes, and they seem to be fairly easy for governments to increase.

Rising Tax Rates

Trying to justify "fairness" but being untruthful and unfair turns everything on its head. This type of deceptive government action is just as tyrannical as any other governmental action that is equally bad. Many patriots might agree to tolerate and accept the penalties of the bad parts of the "Fair Tax" just to get rid of the odious income tax, if it were not for the fact that they know that at any time, any part of the "Fair Tax" can and will be changed by Congress. Historical experience with politic appetites for taxes assures that this will be the case.

A 2000 estimate by Congress's Joint Committee on Taxation found the tax-inclusive rate [such as an income tax rate that takes money from a given amount of wealth] would have to be 36% and the tax-exclusive rate [such as a sale tax rate that adds money to a price to yield a final value] would be 57%. In 2005, the U.S. Treasury Department calculated that a tax-exclusive rate of 34% would be needed just to replace the income tax, leaving the payroll tax in place. But if evasion were high then the rate might have to rise to 49%. If the Fair Tax were only able to cover the limited sales tax base of a typical state, then a rate of 64% would be required (89% with high evasion).

> "*Poverty rates are higher now than in the 1970s, thanks in part to the eroded value of the minimum wage.*"

Raising the Minimum Wage Will Help the Poor

Holly Sklar

Holly Sklar argues in the following viewpoint that the minimum wage in the United States has not kept up with increases in the cost of living. In Sklar's opinion, the minimum wage should be raised to ten dollars an hour by the year 2010. Sklar contends that such a raise will give low-pay workers more consumer power and, in turn, stimulate the economy. She further claims that a raise in the minimum wage will help balance the scale of pay among all workers and therefore keep from widening the gap between the very rich and the very poor. Holly Sklar is the senior policy advisor at Let Justice Roll, a national campaign to raise the minimum wage and reduce poverty.

As you read, consider the following questions:

1. What are the characteristics of a typical minimum wage worker, according to Sklar?

Holly Sklar, "Raise the Minimum Wage to $10 in 2010," *Let Justice Roll Living Wage Campaign*, July 22, 2009. Reproduced by permission. www.letjusticeroll.org.

2. As the author reports, what happened to the unemployment rate between 1995 and 2000 following the minimum wage hikes in 1996 and 1997?

3. In Sklar's view, what should the minimum wage have been in 2008 if it were comparable to the level of the 1950s and 1960s?

The decade between the federal minimum wage increase to $5.15 an hour on Sept. 1, 1997 and the July 24, 2007 increase to $5.85 was the longest period in history without a raise.

• Family health insurance, which cost half a year's minimum wage income in 1998, costs more than the total annual minimum wage today.

Recent minimum wage raises are so little, so late that even with the minimum wage increase on July 24, 2008 to $6.55, workers are still making less than they did in 1997, adjusting for the increased cost of living.

• The 1956 minimum wage is worth $7.93 in today's dollars.

We cannot build a strong 21st economy on 1950s wages.

The minimum wage reached its peak value in 1968. It would take a $9.92 minimum wage today to match the buying power of the minimum wage in 1968—four decadese ago. . . .

$10 in 2010 will bring the minimum wage closer to the value it had in 1968, a year when the unemployment rate was a low 3.6 percent. The next year, unemployment was 3-5%.

A Poverty Wage

The federal minimum wage was enacted in 1938 through the Fair Labor Standards Act, designed to eliminate "labor conditions detrimental to the maintenance of the minimum standard of living necessary for health, efficiency and general well-being of workers."

It is immoral that some are paid so little their children go without necessities—while others are paid so much their grandchildren will live in luxury without having to work at all. . . .

Raising the Minimun Wage Does Not Increase Unemployment

Critics routinely oppose minimum wage increases in good times and bad, claiming they will increase unemployment, no matter the real world record to the contrary. The buying power of the minimum wage reached its peak in 1968. The unemployment rate went from 3.6% in 1968 to 3.5% in 1969

The next time the unemployment rate came close to those levels was after the minimum wage raises of 1996 and 1997. Contrary to what critics predicted when the minimum wage was raised, our economy had unusually low unemployment, high growth, low inflation, and declining poverty rates between 1996 and 2000. The unemployment rate fell from 5.6% in 1995 to 4% in 2000. Unemployment went down across the board across the country—including among people of color, teenagers, high school graduates with no college, and those with less than a high school education.

As *BusinessWeek* put it in 2001, "Many economists have backed away from the argument that minimum wage [laws] lead to fewer jobs."

States that raised their minimum wages above the long stagnant $5.15 federal level experienced better employment and small business trends than states that did not. . . .

Recent studies by the Institute for Research on Labor and Employment (Univ. of CA, Berkeley), carefully controlling for non-minimum wage factors, further advance the extensive research, which shows that minimum wage raises do not cause increased unemployment.

Boosting the Economy

Workers are also consumers. Consumer spending makes up about 70% of our economy.

Minimum wage raises go directly to those who need to spend their increased income on food, housing, healthcare, fuel and other necessities. Minimum wage workers don't put raises into Wall Street's many Ponzi schemes, commodity speculation or offshore tax havens. They recycle their raises back into local businesses and the economy by buying needed goods and services.

According to the Economic Policy Institute's recent report, *A Stealthy Stimulus: How boosting the minimum wage is helping to stimulate the economy*

- The first two minimum wage increases "will have generated an estimated $4.9 billion if spending by July 2009, precisely when our economy needed it the most."

- The July 24, 2009 increase is expected to generate another $5.5 billion over the following year.

In the months leading to the passage of legislation to increase the minimum wage above $5.15, hundreds of business owners and executives—including the CEOs of Costco, the U.S. Women's Chamber of Commerce, and small business owners from every state—signed the Business for a Fair Minimum Wage statement in support of raising the minimum wage. They said, *"We cannot build a strong 21st century economy when more and more hardworking Americans struggle to make ends meet."*

In the words of the business leaders' statement, "Higher wages benefit business by increasing consumer purchasing power, reducing costly employee turnover, raising productivity, and improving product quality, customer satisfaction and company reputation." Decent wages reinforce long-term business success. . . .

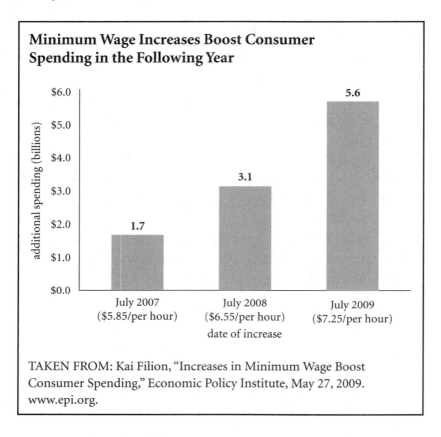

Minimum Wage Increases Boost Consumer Spending in the Following Year

TAKEN FROM: Kai Filion, "Increases in Minimum Wage Boost Consumer Spending," Economic Policy Institute, May 27, 2009. www.epi.org.

Restoring Wage Value

During the 1950s and 60s, the minimum wage averaged around half the average worker wage. The minimum wage was 53% of the average worker wage when it reached peak value in 1968. Before the increase from $5.15 to $5.85 in 2007, the minimum wage had eroded to a record low 30% of the average hourly wage.

• The 2009 average hourly wage is $18.53. Minimum wage would now be $9.82 if it were 53% of that average hourly wage.

Today, more and more two-paycheck households struggle to afford a home, college, healthcare and retirement once normal for middle-class households with one paycheck.

Average wages would be higher now if the minimum wage had reinforced the linkage between wage and productivity growth instead of undermined it.

- Between 1968 and 2008, productivity rose 111%, the average wage fell 3% and the minimum wage fell 34, adjusted for inflation.

What if wages had kept rising with productivity? the average wage—worth $18.68 in 1968 in 2008 dollars—had kept pace with productivity it would be more than $39 today. The minimum wage would be about $20.

We must break the cycle of too little, too late raises.

We must re-link the minimum wage to what people actually need to live on.

We can't build a strong economy on downwardly mobile wages and rising debt and insecurity.

$10 in 2010 will strengthen the foundation under our unstable economy.

Paying workers enough to live on should not be optional—in good times or bad.

Poverty wages are toxic to our families, our communities, our economy, and our democracy. It's time to end them.

> "Common sense says a higher minimum
> wage should fight poverty. The facts,
> however, show otherwise."

Raising the Minimum Wage Will Not Help the Poor

James Sherk

*James Sherk is a fellow in labor policy in the Center for Data
Analysis at the Heritage Foundation, a conservative public policy
research institution. Sherk argues in the following viewpoint that
raising the minimum wage is not an effective strategy to fight
poverty. As Sherk explains, raising the minimum wage will force
employers to cut back hours and offer fewer job positions to low-
income workers. In addition, Sherk says that most minimum-
wage jobs are held by young people who are not from poor
households, and therefore hiking wages will do little for low-
income workers who usually do not possess full-time employment.*

As you read, consider the following questions:

1. What three reasons does Sherk give to support his claim
   that raising the minimum wage does not help eliminate
   poverty?

James Sherk, "Raising the Minimum Wage Will Not Reduce Poverty," Heritage Foundation Backgrounder No. 1994, January 8, 2007. Copyright © 2007 The Heritage Foundation. Reproduced by permission.

2. By what percent does the number of job opportunities for poor people drop for every 10 percent raise in the minimum wage, according to the author?

3. Quoting Census data, what percentage of impoverished workers does Sherk say worked full-time in 2005?

Supporters of raising the minimum wage argue that doing so will reduce poverty. It seems intuitive that raising the minimum wage would have this effect. Presumably, requiring employers to pay their lowest-paid employees more would lift large numbers of low-income households out of poverty. But the evidence shows that this does not happen.

Despite supporters' good intentions, a higher minimum wage will not reduce poverty. This is true for three main reasons.

First, the only workers who benefit from a higher minimum wage are those who actually earn that higher wage. Raising the minimum wage reduces many workers' job opportunities and working hours.

Second, few minimum-wage earners actually come from poor households.

Third, the majority of poor Americans do not work at all, for any wage, so raising the minimum wage does not help them.

Facts Refute Claims

Supporters argue that a higher minimum wage is an effective anti-poverty tool. If businesses must pay their low-wage employees more, then those workers should earn more and fewer of them should live in poverty. Common sense says a higher minimum wage should fight poverty.

The facts, however, show otherwise. Many economists have examined the evidence and come to the surprising conclusion that the minimum wage does not reduce poverty. Ohio University economists Richard Vedder and Lowell Gallaway examined the effect that increases in the minimum wage had on the overall poverty rate in the United States and on the poverty rates for groups like minorities and teenagers that might especially benefit from higher minimum wages. They found that the minimum wage had no statistically detectable effect on poverty rates.

Other researchers have approached the evidence in different ways and reached the same conclusion. For example, economists David Neumark of the University of California–Irvine, Mark Schweitzer of the Federal Reserve Bank of Cleveland, and William Wascher of the Federal Reserve Board examined how the minimum wage affects the incomes of families living near the poverty line. In a series of papers, they repeatedly reached the same conclusion as Vedder and Gallaway: A higher minimum wage does not lift low-income families out of poverty. Their results were particularly clear:

> The answer we obtain to the question of whether minimum wage increases reduce the proportion of poor and low-income families is a fairly resounding "no." The evidence on both family income distributions and changes in incomes experienced by families indicates that minimum wages raise the incomes of some poor families, but that their net effect is to increase the portion of families that are poor and near-poor.

Whether measured by the poverty rate or by the earnings of low-income families, the minimum wage does not help the poor.

A Cost in Jobs and Working Hours

A major reason why the minimum wage is such an ineffective anti-poverty tool is that minimum-wage hikes cause businesses to reduce the number of workers they hire and the hours they ask their employees to work. According to Neumark *et al.*, for example:

Wage Raise Cuts Benefits

Even when minimum-wage increases don't put low-wage workers out of work, they don't necessarily help them either. The reason: Employers respond to forced higher wages by adjusting other components of employee compensation, such as health insurance or other benefits. Although few minimum wage workers have employer-provided health insurance, employers have found other ways to adjust, such as cutting on-the-job training. In their study of changes in the minimum-wage laws between 1981 and 1991, [economist David] Neumark and Federal Reserve Board member and economist William Wascher concluded, "[M]inimum wages reduce training aimed at improving skills on the current job, especially formal training."

David R. Henderson,
National Center for Policy Analysis,
Brief Analysis No. 550, May 4, 2006.

Workers who initially earn near the minimum wage experience wage gains. But their hours and employment decline, and the combined effect of these changes on earned income suggests net adverse consequences for low-wage workers.

Most estimates suggest that each 10 percent increase in the minimum wage reduces employment in affected groups of workers by roughly 2 percent. Thus, raising the minimum wage to $7.25 an hour would cost at least 8 percent of affected workers their jobs. A higher minimum wage helps only those workers who actually wind up earning that wage and further disadvantages lower-income workers, who suffer fewer job opportunities and working hours. Though intended to help low-income families get ahead, the minimum wage instead costs some their jobs and others hours at work. This leaves poor families actually worse off.

Few Minimum-Wage Workers Are Poor

Another reason for the failure of higher minimum wages to reduce poverty is that the vast majority of minimum-wage workers do not live in poverty. Much of the benefit of a higher minimum wage accrues to suburban teenagers and college students, not the heads of poor families. A majority of minimum-wage earners are between the ages of 16 and 24, and over three-fifths of minimum-wage earners work part-time. The average family income of a minimum-wage earner is almost $50,000, and less than one in five live at or below the poverty line.

It therefore should not be surprising that higher minimum wages do little to benefit poor families when minimum-wage workers are only slightly more likely to be poor than is the population as a whole.

Members of Poor Families Work Less

Higher minimum wages do not address the main reason that most poor families live below the poverty line. Contrary to what many assume, low wages are not the primary problem, because most poor Americans do not work for the minimum wage. The problem is that most poor Americans do not work at all. . . .

[As Census data reveal], over three-fifths of individuals living below the poverty line [in 2005] did not work, and only 11 percent worked full-time year-round. Families are poor not because they earn low wages but because they do not have full-time jobs. The median family with children living below the poverty line works only 1,040 hours a year in total. That is only 20 hours per week. If at least one parent in every poor household worked full-time year-round, the child poverty rate in the United States would plummet by 72 percent. Raising the minimum wage does not address this problem and, by causing businesses to hire fewer workers, actually makes it harder for potential workers to find full-time jobs.

An Ineffective Solution

Extensive research shows that the minimum wage does little to reduce poverty. While this may appear counterintuitive, deeper analysis reveals three reasons behind the minimum wage's ineffectiveness.

First, a higher minimum wage causes employers to cut back on both the number of workers they hire and their employees' working hours.

Second, the beneficiaries of higher minimum wages are unlikely to be poor because most minimum-wage earners are not poor.

Finally, few individuals living in poverty work at minimum-wage jobs or any job.

For all its advocates' good intentions, raising the minimum wage will not reduce poverty in America.

Periodical Bibliography

The following articles have been selected to supplement the diverse views presented in this chapter.

Matthew Bandyk   "A Plan to Junk the Income Tax," Interview, *U.S. News & World Report*, April 14, 2008.

Geoff Colvin   "The Tax Debate We Should Be Having," *Fortune*, April 14, 2008.

Laura Fitzpatrick   "Brief History: The Minimum Wage," *Time*, August 3, 2009.

Steve Forbes   "The U.S. Income Tax: Start Over!" *Forbes Global*, June 6, 2005.

David Frum   "The Vanishing Republican Voter," *New York Times*, September 5, 2008.

Clara Jeffery   "A Look at the Numbers: How the Rich Get Richer," *Mother Jones*, May/June 2006.

James Pethokoukis   "The Income Gap," *U.S. News & World Report*, January 22, 2007.

Virginia Postrel   "Inconspicuous Consumption: A New Theory of the Leisure Class," *Atlantic Monthly*, July/August 2008.

Gerry Roll   "Understanding Poverty and Homelessness in America," *Christian Science Monitor*, May 22, 2006.

Dirk Van Dijk   "All Men Created Economically Unequal," *Daily Markets*, August 14, 2009.

OPPOSING
VIEWPOINTS®
SERIES

CHAPTER 2

What Policies Would Promote Social Justice for Minorities?

Chapter Preface

The passage of the Civil Rights Act of 1964 rendered racial segregation and exclusion by race or gender from schools, employment, and public places illegal. While the Civil Rights Act did not end all forms of discrimination, American attitudes toward race changed over the next forty-five years. Social critics, however, still debate whether these attitudes have changed enough to ensure social justice for racial and ethnic minorities.

In 2008, when the U.S. electorate elected Barack Obama, the nation's first nonwhite president, to lead the nation, some observers assumed that his administration would symbolize America's transition to a "post-racial" society. They hoped that problems arising from racial inequality would be resolved by the mere fact that a biracial man held the nation's highest office. Yet critics were skeptical that an election could usher in such an immediate change. As Tomás Jiménez of the New America Foundation, a public policy institute, put it, "The problem with viewing the most recent historical event as a clean shift from Before Obama to After Obama is that we fail to see just how much race still defines inequality." During the same year that Barack Obama took the oath of office, statistics reported grim realities. Black families were three times more likely to live in poverty than white families, and black adults were twice as likely to be unemployed than white adults. Black men composed 6 percent of the population, yet made up 37 percent of prison inmates, making them seven times more likely to be jailed than white men. The list of unbalanced outcomes seemed nearly endless.

Although inequalities exist, polls show that America is changing. A *New York Times*/CBS poll in 2009 found that 59 percent of blacks and 65 percent of whites cast race relations in America as "good." Perhaps more revealing, a Gallup poll indicated that a large number of Americans—both black and white—believe that racial discrimination is often used as an excuse for personal failure. According to this line of thought, people of color might claim that racial discrimination is hindering them in order to avoid responsibility for underachievement. In an editorial for the *New York Times*, Brent Staples noted that successful blacks are often touted as examples that racial discrimination is in decline in America and that all people are availing themselves of the opportunities afforded in society. Striking a cautionary note, however, Staples writes, "In this rhetoric of race, there is no such thing as social disadvantage, only hard-working, morally upright people who succeed, and lazy, morally defective people who do not."

In 2004, black comedian Bill Cosby ignited a controversy when he scolded lower-income blacks for not attending to their children's education. His comments seemed to support Staples' claims. Responding to Cosby, former director of the National Association for the Advancement of Colored People Legal Defense Fund Theodore M. Shaw framed the issues as more economic than racial, saying, "As a nation, we wage war on poor people in this country, not on poverty." He pointed out, "Many of the problems Cosby addressed are largely a function of concentrated poverty in black communities—the legacy of centuries of governmental and private neglect and discrimination."

The viewpoints in the following chapter address several proposed solutions to the problems of race-based and sexual inequality. Whether and how these proposals will effect public policy is yet to be seen.

| "Affirmative action . . . is a vital part of public policy advancing equal opportunity."

Affirmative Action Programs Promote Equal Opportunity

Ari Melber

In the following viewpoint, Ari Melber claims that affirmative action programs are in danger of being dismissed in an era in which Americans have come to believe that racial preferences are no longer needed or even counterproductive. Melber asserts that the presidential candidacy of Barack Obama plays into this widely held belief because his political rise seems to be based on his merits and not his race. But Melber argues that Obama's rise—as well as the advancement of other minority political leaders—owes a lot to the affirmative action policies that aided these individuals by giving them the opportunity to prove themselves in academic institutions that did provide a leg up for minorities. Melber maintains that more qualified, effective minority leaders are needed to change the nation's current power structure, and that affirmative action policies should be retained to ensure that tomorrow's leaders will truly represent America's cherished diversity. Ari Melber is a public affairs correspondent for the Nation *magazine.*

As you read, consider the following questions:

1. What evidence does Melber give to support his claim that America may be willing to sweep aside the gains made by policies designed to redress racial discrimination?

2. Why does the author think that focusing affirmative action on creating "diversity" was an abuse of the policy's original aims?

3. Why does Melber state that President George W. Bush refused to "preach what he practiced" when it came to affirmative action?

In America's long struggle for racial equality, 2007 was a paradoxical year. Just as our political system seriously contemplated a black President for the very first time, the Supreme Court declared the end of racial integration policy, halting voluntary local remedies to desegregate public schools under *Brown v. Board of Education*. Presented with the rise of Barack Obama and the fall of *Brown*, most people have focused on the good news.

Many Americans were captivated by the self-proclaimed "audacity" of Obama's January [2007] announcement that he was running for President. Obama made it clear he was not running to send a message or to register voters but literally to get elected. His campaign initially worked because the political elites accepted this unprecedented proposition. Reporters took Obama's candidacy seriously from its inception, and the donors did, too. Obama has already secured more than a footnote in history, shattering records for individual contributors to his campaign. Win or lose, he is arguably the first black American to be treated by the political and media establishment as a fully viable presidential contender. It is an achievement that cannot be claimed by any other racial minorities. (Jesse Jackson's campaigns did not attain such standing with the political establishment, despite their significance for many voters.) We should not gloss over this development. It is a meaningful step towards addressing a resilient, uncomfortable American fact: our national power structure has always been, and stubbornly remains, overwhelmingly white, from all forty-three Presidents across history to ninety-five of the one hundred senators serving today.

The Move to Ban Affirmative Action

That segregated power structure was reinforced by the Supreme Court's sharply divided June decision to ban integration programs in public schools. Most educational policies that consider a student's race for the purposes of integration are now illegal. Like the original *Brown* opinion, [2007]'s decision is not neatly confined to K-12 schools, either. *Brown* consecrated a new national ambition for racial equality in the public sphere, delegitimizing both explicit and implicit racism in government, and laying a foundation for remedial measures to equalize many other facets of our society. Many critics contend that this case, *Parents Involved In Community Schools v. Seattle School District No. 1*, augurs a disturbing slide backwards. It bans integration programs, sharply restricts race-based government remedies and sets the stage for future bans on other remedial programs, such as affirmative action, as Justice Stephen Breyer warned.

But will the public really stand for this sweeping attack on *Brown*'s legacy?

Yes. In most of the country, public opposition towards measures to remedy America's history of racial discrimination, from academic recruitment to professional affirmative action, has actually outpaced the conservative court. Even putting aside the South, generally liberal electorates—including California, Washington and Michigan—have passed state referenda completely banning affirmative action. Hostility towards affirmative action runs so deep, in fact, it is a staple of attacks against black political candidates. [Former North Carolina] Senator Jesse Helms perfected coded campaign racism in 1990, with an infamous attack ad darkly juxtaposing his black opponent's face with the text "For RACIAL QUOTAS." Which brings us back to Barack Obama.

Exceptional Black Success Story

Some commentators have latched onto Obama's success as proof for the flawed claim that the United States has completely achieved equal opportunity for all, obviating remedial programs like affirmative action. "Obama embodies and preaches the true and vital message that in today's America, the opportunities available to black people are *unlimited if* they work hard, play by the rules, and get a good education," writes Stuart Taylor Jr., a columnist for the *National Journal* (emphasis added). Taylor presents one man's unusual political arc as a universal lesson for all "black children": "Obama's soaring success should tell black children everywhere that they, too, can succeed, and they do not need handouts or reparations." Obama's success is definitely inspirational, but is that because it is an average example or a remarkable exception?

As a politician, Obama is an accomplished black man who knows that some voters still see him, before all else, as "the black candidate." It seems as if commentators either fixate on how his blackness makes his candidacy historic—as I just did—or debate whether he is "black enough." Obama dutifully protests these lines of inquiry, assuring audiences that his qualifications, vision and personal experiences transcend race. This is not only true, it is a political necessity. Obama knows that he is unlikely to win as the "black candidate," let alone the "affirmative-action candidate."

Few other campaigns in recent memory have pressed meritocratic credentials as forcefully as Obama's aides. Today's candidates tend to downplay their Ivy League educations in favor of more humble qualifications. Yet it is rare to hear Obama's history discussed without a reference to Harvard, or his prestigious stint as editor-in-chief of its *Law Review*. Even when his campaign is not emphasizing it, reporters highlight Obama's education far more than any other candidate's. Take, for example, articles from the major newspapers about the leading Democratic candidates in the first ten months of [2007]'s campaign. Obama's Harvard Law credentials turn up a whopping 178 times—six times the thirty Yale references for [Democratic candidate] Hillary Clinton. [Democratic candidate] John Edwards's law school was only mentioned once, in an article about how he met his wife.

This emphasis is vital to Obama's candidacy. He earned his past success and current prominence, in this narrative, as evidenced by his academic achievement and intelligence. The story line aims to banish the racist thought, lurking beneath our public discourse, that perhaps this candidate succeeded only because of his race. Sometimes it seeps out anyway. During a January [2007] appearance on Fox News, columnist John McWhorter offered the baseless claim that "the reason that [Obama is] considered such a big deal is simply because he's black." McWhorter implausibly continued, "If you took away the color of his skin, nobody right now would be paying him any attention."

An Opportunity to Prove Oneself

Such baseless attacks obviously predate Barack Obama. Even the most extraordinarily successful minorities are either attacked for their achievements, or the meaning of their educational and professional advancement is contested. Like other talented, smart and successful black Americans who have broken barriers (including [former secretaries of state] Colin

Drops in Minority Enrollments

California [is] a state that has been without affirmative action for more than 10 years. . . .

At Berkeley the combined enrollments of Hispanic, black, and American Indian students topped 20 percent of the student body before Proposition 209, the 1996 ballot measure that prohibited public institutions from considering race, sex, or ethnicity in admissions. The best that Berkeley has been able to achieve since Prop 209 was passed is 14 percent. Similarly, the share of the enrollment of underrepresented minority students at the University of California at Los Angeles has dropped from more than 30 percent before Prop 209 to less than 20 percent today.

Those losses have occurred in an environment in which, nationally, Hispanic and black students are increasing both in numbers and as a share of the total enrollment in higher education.

Michele S. Moses, Patricia Marin, and John T. Yun,
Chronicle of Higher Education, *October 10, 2008.*

Powell and Condoleezza Rice), Obama excelled in an institution that used affirmative action to propel qualified minority applicants. Having proven their mettle as leaders, it is clear each of these figures would excel without affirmative action. And no one knows how their careers would have developed in a society without remedial measures for discrimination. Yet their paths show how the United States has benefited from applying affirmative action in public institutions.

Rice has emphasized how affirmative action gave her an opportunity to prove herself in academia. "I myself am the beneficiary of a Stanford strategy that took affirmative action seriously," she told a Stanford faculty meeting in 1997, and her rise through academia and government embodies the policy's four original rationales: minority students can overcome adversity, excel academically, share their perspectives to enrich a diverse student body and benefit from the requisite training for leadership positions in society, eventually helping to redress the effects of hundreds of years of discrimination. In other words, by pursuing the values of adversity, diversity and redress on campus, universities can both improve their educational offering and advance equality across American society. Americans are decidedly mixed on "affirmative action"—both as a literal program and as a vessel for complex emotions about race—but few would openly challenge those values. Yet those values have not driven the debate for a long time.

Touting Diversity Was a Mistake

In 1978, the Supreme Court struck down a University of California affirmative action program and rejected most of the program's traditional rationales. Adversity and redress were out. Instead, Justice Lewis Powell carved out narrow legal authority for programs advancing "diversity," based on the university's special First Amendment right to foster diverse and open educational environments. "The atmosphere of speculation, experiment and creation—so essential to the quality of higher education—is widely believed to be promoted by a diverse student body," he declared.

The opinion would have profound "discourse shaping effects," as Yale Law School Professor Jack Balkin has written, because advocates of affirmative action could no longer defend the program's legality by citing illegal rationales. So an administrator might support affirmative action because people who overcome adversity have qualities that tests do not reflect, or because redressing a history of racist exclusion enhances the institution's legitimacy, but those arguments were suddenly out of bounds. The courts specifically required "diversity" to justify affirmative action.

Depicting affirmative action solely as a diversity measure not only departs from the program's original purposes. It is also a tough sell. For example, when a 2003 Gallup poll simply asked white Americans whether they "favor" affirmative action, 44 percent said yes and 49 percent said no. When the same poll offered a more detailed choice between college affirmative action "to help promote diversity" or admissions operating "solely on the basis of merit," however, white support for affirmative action plummeted 20 points. Blacks and Hispanics, who favored affirmative action by higher margins, also backed off in this question, with support dropping 21 and 27 points, respectively. Severed from other rationales and pitted against merit, it turns out that even for sympathetic Americans, "diversity" is a drag on affirmative action's validity. Apparently the public imagination prefers bootstrap narratives to the gauzy diversity of Benetton ads.

Building Good Leaders

It took another twenty-five years for the Supreme Court to move beyond its cramped conception of diversity as the only acceptable rationale for affirmative action. In 2003, the Court broadened the legal foundation for the policy. In a five-to-four decision, the Court cited an influential amicus brief from one of the most aggressive proponents of affirmative action, the US military. A group of former Defense Secretaries and Chairmen of the Joint Chiefs [of Staff] explained that beyond the largely intrinsic benefit of diversity, the very legitimacy and efficacy of the military was advanced when its leadership looked like the rest of the enlisted soldiers. The brief declared that a "highly qualified, racially diverse officer corps educated and trained to command our nation's racially diverse enlisted ranks is essential." The Supreme Court largely adopted that view, through Justice [Sandra Day] O'Connor's majority opinion, touting the importance of diverse national leadership for the entire country:

[U]niversities, and in particular, law schools, represent the training ground for a large number of our Nation's leaders. Individuals with law degrees occupy roughly half the state governorships, more than half the seats in the United States Senate, and more than a third of the seats in the United States House of Representatives. The pattern is even more striking when it comes to highly selective law schools. A handful of these schools accounts for 25 of the 100 United States Senators, 74 United States Courts of Appeals judges, and nearly 200 of the more than 600 United States District Court judges. In order to cultivate a set of leaders with legitimacy in the eyes of the citizenry, it is necessary that the path to leadership be visibly open to talented and qualified individuals of every race and ethnicity. All members of our heterogeneous society must have confidence in the openness and integrity of the educational institutions that provide this training.

Thus the Court finally conceded that programs ensuring minorities have access to education and power are important for public legitimacy and redressing past discrimination. After all, the lack of "diversity" among today's leaders is a product of historical discrimination. (The discrimination ranges from the obvious, like voter suppression, to the obscure, like college legacy preferences that function as grandfather clauses for mostly white alumni.) The Court still talked about diversity, since it was the only accepted rationale within the relevant precedent, but it became a vessel for other, underlying grounds that had been pushed off the stage.

Bush's Use of Affirmative Action

This "diversity in national leadership" approach also received an important boost from an unlikely benefactor: George W. Bush.

Liberals and conservatives rarely discuss it, but Bush applied affirmative action to select his cabinet, elevating more racial minorities to senior positions than any administration in American history. That includes, of course, two secretaries of state, (officially the highest-ranking cabinet post), a national security adviser, an attorney general and the secretaries of commerce, labor, transportation and housing and urban development. Contrarians might claim that all those barriers were broken by accident, in a colorblind process that just happened to make history.

Yet the record reveals Bush's deliberate use of affirmative action. Bush went out of his way to find black candidates in a Republican Party [GOP] that grooms virtually no black politicians for the national stage. (There are no black Republican members of Congress, and only seven percent of black Americans self-identify as Republicans, according to a 2004 study by the Pew Research Center.) Finding qualified black leaders required a rare detour from the GOP's overwhelmingly white, partisan networks. It is no surprise that the President tapped the two American institutions at the forefront of affirmative action, the military and the academy, to select former general Powell and former provost Rice.

Why doesn't Bush get more credit for using affirmative action to build the most diverse cabinet in American history?

He refused to preach what he practiced.

In a conservative twist on "politically correct" culture, Republicans often banish the language of affirmative action even when they practice it. While Bush consciously recruited minorities into some of the most important positions in the United States, he would not admit it. Instead, he spoke out against affirmative action, claiming to advocate only "race-neutral" programs, and thrust his Solicitor General into the odd position of arguing against the President's own policies in the 2003 affirmative action case before the Supreme Court.

Affirmative Action Still Needed

The Administration lost, of course, in the decision written by Justice O'Connor. Now she has been replaced by Samuel Alito, who is widely expected to be the fifth vote for banning all affirmative action at the next opportunity. After all, the [Chief Justice John] Roberts Court was not shy about taking the earliest chance to undermine *Brown*, a unanimous opinion celebrated as a zenith for the Court's civil rights accomplishments. The legal precedents for affirmative action are weaker, stretched between Justice Powell's plurality and Justice O'Connor's retired swing vote. Meanwhile, the political branches offer little solace, since even politicians who use affirmative action often dare not speak its name, and many now stress their support for preferences based on class, instead of race. Of course, class-based affirmative action, like financial-need scholarships, is a vital part of public policy advancing equal opportunity. But it cannot replace measures that directly address our history of legal, political and educational discrimination.

Ultimately, one part of the high public regard for bright, talented successful black leaders like Obama, Rice or Powell stems from public awareness that our country is still struggling to overcome racial barriers. Powell earned his success within a military and a Cabinet that proudly used affirmative action not simply as a benefit for individual "applicants" like him, not only as a "diversity" boost for his peers in military and government circles, but as an extrinsic value for the progress of our nation and the legitimacy of its leadership. As the first top-tier black presidential candidate, Obama has already advanced that progress another step. Yet win or lose, such examples remain too rare, as the first post-civil rights era cohort [statistical group] comes of age. Even Obama's potential election reveals this trend, for his elevation to the White House would leave the Senate without a single black member. We still need affirmative action in college, government and business—animated by race, class and equal opportunity—if we are ever going to reform America's resiliently segregated power structure.

> "Affirmative action, whether under the
> name of quotas or diversity, does more
> harm than good."

Affirmative Action Programs Do Not Promote Equal Opportunity

Gary Becker

In the following viewpoint, Gary Becker, a professor of economics at the University of Chicago and a senior fellow at the Hoover Institution, dismisses the need for affirmative action programs in the United States. Becker claims that American society is a meritocracy and that no one should be granted special privileges in the job market or in education due to race, ethnicity, or gender. In Becker's opinion, affirmative action may help disadvantaged individuals place in universities and businesses, but because these people are often less qualified than their majority peers, they end up performing poorly in relation to these peers. While this does nothing to better the self-esteem of the minority student or worker, it also makes the rejected but qualified majority applicants feel as though they were cheated out of an opportunity they deserved, Becker argues. Becker believes the appropriate solution is for schools and businesses to work harder in their search

Gary Becker, "On Affirmative Action," Becker-Posner Blog, August 21, 2005. Reproduced by permission.

for qualified minority candidates—not to lower the standards by giving special consideration to all disadvantaged minorities.

As you read, consider the following questions:

1. What examples does Becker give of affirmative action programs lowering the standards for minority admissions and promotions in business and academia?

2. According to an example the author gives, how are some minorities directly hurt by affirmative action policies in the business world?

3. Why does Becker believe many minority doctors and other professionals are looked on "suspiciously" by patients and customers?

Arguments about affirmative action, and its offshoots, diversity and quotas, bring out almost as much passion as arguments over abortion. Passion usually replaces reasoned analysis, so I will try to discuss as objectively as I can why I oppose practically all the major forms of affirmative action in place now at universities, the political sector, and businesses in the United States, Western Europe, and many other countries in all regions of the world.

Catering to Special Interests

Let me say at the outset that I view affirmative action programs as mainly catering to special interest groups, in the same way as quotas on imports of agricultural goods cater to domestic farming interests. To be sure, affirmative action programs are defended with attractive language, such as that they are designed to offset the harm of past discrimination, or that they are simply trying to level the playing field for persons of different races, genders, or ethnicities. But all special interests programs are typically defended with nice-sounding language, such as that agricultural support is necessary to preserve the rural way of life, or that American ownership of energy resources is necessary for national security reasons, or that subsidies to small businesses [are] necessary to prevent predatory actions by large companies. I also want to stress that though I oppose affirmative actions, I believe that many other special interest programs, such as various aspects of the social security system, subsidies to agriculture, restrictions on immigration of skilled workers, and the presently developed tort system, do far more economic and social damage than does affirmative action.

Most affirmative action programs, disguised or openly, use lower standards for African Americans and members of various other minority groups than for white males in determining whether they are promoted to higher level jobs in private business or government, admitted to better universities, and in other situations. Universities have openly used affirmative action by lowering substantially the acceptable SAT score for African Americans (and certain other groups) seeking admission compared to the scores required for whites or Asians. A disguised way, adopted by some states, is to admit applicants to state universities and colleges if they rank in the top 10 per cent of their high school class. This is disguised affirmative action because schools with favored minority groups typically have much worse students than other schools, so it is considerably easier to rank in the top 10 per cent of the lower quality, mainly minority schools.

American Society Should Be a Meritocracy

It is obvious why affirmative action may hurt members of the majority group who are denied promotions or admission to various colleges, even though their records are better than many minorities accepted. But why is it bad for a country like the United States to do this, and often also for the minority groups gaining these privileges? My belief is that affirmative action is bad for any country that aspires to be a meritocracy, as the United States does, despite past slavery and discrimination that are terrible violations of this aspiration. The case for a meritocracy is that achievement based on merit produces the most dynamic, innovative, and flexible economy and social structure. Encouraging promotion or admission of less qualified applicants because of their race, gender, or other characteristics, clearly violates this principle, and produces a less progressive economy, and a distorted social structure.

The appeal of a meritocracy explains why one can, as I do, strongly oppose both affirmative action, and discrimination against African Americans, women, and various other groups that have suffered discrimination in employment and in admissions to schools and colleges. While affirmative action programs give advantages to various minorities that are not justified by qualifications, discrimination does the opposite, and gives advantages to the majority that exceed their skills and qualifications. Unfortunately, laws opposing discrimination against various minorities often evolve into affirmative action laws, where the test of discrimination is not whether better-qualified minorities are passed over for jobs and promotions, but whether firms and universities have a sufficient number of members of designated minorities. Political pressure also has extended discrimination laws to groups that have suffered little in the past from discrimination, such as older workers. It is hard to sympathize from a discrimination viewpoint with older workers since they typically earn much more and have much lower unemployment rates than young workers, they easily qualify for decent disability income, and they can retire relatively early to receive taxpayer-supported retirement and medical benefits.

No Redress for Past Injustices

Affirmative action is often justified as making up to African Americans, American Indians, and some other groups for the terrible discrimination and treatment they received in the past. Some affirmative action advocates argue that giving preference to minority applicants at colleges is no different from legacies—that is, giving preferences to children of alumni. Perhaps legacies have been overused, and their use is declining at the top universities, but the objective case for them is that this makes for more loyal and generous alumni. In addition, a good school record of a relative may be a useful predictor of an applicant's school record.

I am not trying to minimize the terrible treatment especially of African-Americans in the past. I am questioning whether affirmative action programs make up for past injustices. Clearly, some members of favored groups benefit from affirmative action, but others are hurt in direct and not so direct ways. To consider a direct way, many companies try to avoid hiring minorities favored by affirmative action because they realize they may face lawsuits in the future if they do not promote them, even when the promotions are not justified. Their refusal to hire because of affirmative action pressures later on makes them subject to anti-discrimination legislation, which is one way that laws against discrimination evolve into affirmative action.

Creating Disadvantages

A more subtle way that affirmative action harms many members of the very groups they are trying to promote is illustrated by admissions to college. If lower admission standards are used to admit African Americans or other groups, then good colleges would accept average minority students, good minority students would be accepted by very good colleges, and quite good students would be accepted by the most outstanding universities, like Harvard or Stanford. This means that at all these types of schools, the qualifications of minority students would on average be below those of other students. As a result, they tend to rank at the lower end of their classes, even when they are good students, because affirmative action

"It's nothing personal, Osgood —
We're letting you go as part of
our affirmative action program."

"It's nothing personal, Osgood — We're letting you go as part of our affirmative action program," by Rex May Baloo. www.CartoonStock.com.

makes them compete against even better students. Studies have shown that this simple implication of affirmative action applies to students at good law schools, where the average African American student ranks toward the lower end of their law school cohort [statistically similar group]. My observation of many colleges and universities is that this conclusion has general applicability well beyond law schools.

It hardly helps self-esteem if one is a member of a group that typically ranks toward the bottom in performance at a university or on a job. When discrimination dominated affirmative action, an African American or female medical doctor would be better than average since they had to overcome artificial hurdles to get where they were. That was not a desirable situation because discrimination made it harder for these groups to get ahead, so fewer of them than was warranted by their abilities and skills managed to make it to medical school. However, now, minority doctors and other professionals are greeted suspiciously by many patients and customers who fear they got where they are only because they were subject to lower standards. That can hardly make someone feel good, and helps explain some of the segregation and defensiveness of minorities receiving affirmative action help at schools or on jobs.

Alternative Ways to Help

While opposing affirmative action, I do not advocate just letting the status quo operate without attempting to help groups that have suffered greatly in the past from discrimination. Employers, universities, and other organizations should make special efforts to find qualified members of minority groups, persons who might have been overlooked because of their poor family backgrounds or the bad schools they attended. By using this approach, one can spot some diamonds in the rough that would get overlooked. I know that the economics department at [the University of] Chicago in recent years has been able to discover and help train some excellent economists from disadvantaged backgrounds by searching harder for them.

Another attractive policy is to help disadvantaged children at early ages rather than using affirmative action when they apply for jobs or colleges. There is still controversy over how much and how durable is the gain from head start programs, although I believe that extra effort spent on these children at very young ages tends to yield a decent return in terms of later achievements. But it has been conclusively shown that efforts to educate and help in other ways when children are in their teens generally fail since by that time the children have fallen too far behind others of their age to be able to catch up. Put more technically, current human capital investment builds on past investments, so if past investments are inadequate, the current investments have low returns.

My concluding comment is that affirmative action is too often confused with anti-discrimination action. I believe there should be vigorous prosecution of discrimination toward groups like African Americans that have suffered from substantial discrimination. I also support positive efforts to bring children from minority groups closer to the achievement levels of others. However, affirmative action, whether under the name of quotas or diversity, does more harm than good, even though it is not the worst form of interest group politics.

> *"I believe that, when my daughters grow up, barriers to marriage equality for same-sex couples will seem as archaic, and as unfair, as the laws we once had against inter-racial marriage."*

Gay Marriage Promotes Equality

Chris Dodd

Chris Dodd is a U.S. senator and Democrat from Connecticut. He is a senior member of the Health, Education, Labor, and Pensions Committee and is the chairman of its Children and Families Subcommittee. In the following viewpoint, Dodd argues that gay marriage should be accepted in the United States. In Dodd's view, gay partners who want to marry are simply expressing the same love and commitment that binds heterosexual couples. Dodd claims that the United States has progressed and that society must keep pace to ensure that justice and equality apply to all citizens.

As you read, consider the following questions:

1. Why does Dodd think that many Americans have a difficult time accepting gay marriage?

Chris Dodd, "Rights, Responsibilities and Love," *Meriden* (Connecticut) *Record-Journal*, June 21, 2009.

2. What does the author want his children to remember about him in the struggle to make gay marriage legal and accepted?

3. What other LGBT issues does Dodd say that he has supported?

Public officials aren't supposed to change their minds. But I firmly believe that it's important to keep learning. Last week [in June 2009], while I was in Connecticut meeting with members of the gay and lesbian community from across the state, I had the opportunity to tell them what I've learned about marriage, and about equality.

While I've long been for extending every benefit of marriage to same-sex couples, I have in the past drawn a distinction between a marriage-like status ("civil unions") and full marriage rights.

The reason was simple: I was raised to believe that marriage is between a man and a woman. And as many other Americans have realized as they've struggled to reconcile the principle of fairness with the lessons they learned early in life, that's not an easy thing to overcome.

But the fact that I was raised a certain way just isn't a good enough reason to stand in the way of fairness anymore.

Society Changing for the Better

The Connecticut Supreme Court, of course, has ruled that such a distinction holds no merit under the law. And the Court is right.

I believe that effective leaders must be able and willing to grow and change over their service. I certainly have during mine—and so has the world. Thirty-five years ago, who could have imagined that we'd have an African-American President of the United States?

My young daughters are growing up in a different reality than I did. Our family knows many same-sex couples—our

"Gay Marriage Debate," by Justin Bilicki, www.CartoonStock.com.

neighbors in Connecticut, members of my staff, parents of their schoolmates. Some are now married because the Connecticut Supreme Court and our state legislature have made same-sex marriage legal in our state.

But to my daughters, these couples are married simply because they love each other and want to build a life together. That's what we've taught them. The things that make those families different from their own pale in comparison to the commitments that bind those couples together.

And, really, that's what marriage should be. It's about rights and responsibilities and, most of all, love.

Standing for What Is Right

I believe that, when my daughters grow up, barriers to marriage equality for same-sex couples will seem as archaic, and as unfair, as the laws we once had against inter-racial marriage.

And I want them to know that, even if he was a little late, their dad came down on the right side of history.

I have always been proud of my long record fighting for the civil rights of the LGBT [lesbian, gay, bisexual, and transgender] community. I've co-sponsored legislation to strengthen hate crime laws and end discrimination in the workplace. I've spoken out against [the military's policy of] "don't ask, don't tell" and always supported equal rights for domestic partnerships.

But I am also proud to now count myself among the many elected officials, advocates, and ordinary citizens who support full marriage equality for same-sex couples.

I understand that even those who oppose discrimination might continue to find it hard to re-think the definition of marriage they grew up with. I know it was for me.

But many of the things we must do to make our union more perfect—whether it's fighting for decades to reform our health care system or struggling with a difficult moral question—are hard. They take time. And they require that, when you come to realize that something is right, you be unafraid to stand up and say it.

That's the only way our history will progress along that long arc towards justice.

> "Changing the meaning of marriage to accommodate homosexual orientation further and perhaps definitively undermines . . . marriage's most distinctive contribution to human society."

Gay Marriage Harms Society

David Blankenhorn

In the following viewpoint, David Blankenhorn claims that he rejects homophobia, but he does not support gay marriage. In Blankenhorn's view, marriage is an institution established to further procreation. He believes that all children have a birthright to know and be cared for by the two parents who brought them into the world. Gay marriage, as Blankenhorn attests, deprives children of this birthright, and while it may help adults feel more tolerant, it does nothing to salve the wound to the children. Blankenhorn maintains that if society values its children, it must reject the notion of gay marriage. David Blankenhorn is the president of the Institute for American Values, a nonprofit organization that seeks to shape policy making on marriage and the family.

David Blankenhorn, "Protecting Marriage to Protect Children," *Los Angeles Times*, September 19, 2008. Copyright © 2008 Los Angeles Times. Reproduced by permission.

As you read, consider the following questions:

1. What is the one constant within the evolving conception of marriage through human history, according to Blankenhorn?

2. As the author relates, what did Child Trends researchers conclude in their 2002 report on family structure?

3. As Blankenhorn claims, what relevant right is specifically guaranteed in the United Nations Convention on the Rights of the Child?

I'm a liberal Democrat. And I do not favor same-sex marriage. Do those positions sound contradictory? To me, they fit together.

Many seem to believe that marriage is simply a private love relationship between two people. They accept this view, in part, because Americans have increasingly emphasized and come to value the intimate, emotional side of marriage, and in part because almost all opinion leaders today, from journalists to judges, strongly embrace this position. That's certainly the idea that underpinned the California Supreme Court's legalization of same-sex marriage.

But I spent a year studying the history and anthropology of marriage, and I've come to a different conclusion.

Marriage Is About Children

Marriage as a human institution is constantly evolving, and many of its features vary across groups and cultures. But there is one constant. In all societies, marriage shapes the rights and obligations of parenthood. Among us humans, the scholars report, marriage is not primarily a license to have sex. Nor is it primarily a license to receive benefits or social recognition. It is primarily a license to have children.

In this sense, marriage is a gift that society bestows on its next generation. Marriage (and only marriage) unites the three core dimensions of parenthood—biological, social and legal—into one pro-child form: the married couple. Marriage says to a child: The man and the woman whose sexual union made you will also be there to love and raise you. Marriage says to society as a whole: For every child born, there is a recognized mother and a father, accountable to the child and to each other.

These days, because of the gay marriage debate, one can be sent to bed without supper for saying such things. But until very recently, almost no one denied this core fact about marriage. Summing up the cross-cultural evidence, the anthropologist Helen Fisher in 1992 put it simply: "People wed primarily to reproduce." The philosopher and Nobel laureate Bertrand Russell, certainly no friend of conventional sexual morality, was only repeating the obvious a few decades earlier when he concluded that "it is through children alone that sexual relations become important to society, and worthy to be taken cognizance of by a legal institution."

Marriage is society's most pro-child institution. In 2002—just moments before it became highly unfashionable to say so—a team of researchers from Child Trends, a nonpartisan research center, reported that "family structure clearly matters for children, and the family structure that helps children the most is a family headed by two biological parents in a low-conflict marriage."

All our scholarly instruments seem to agree: For healthy development, what a child needs more than anything else is the mother and father who together made the child, who love the child and love each other.

Children Have a Birthright

For these reasons, children have the right, insofar as society can make it possible, to know and to be cared for by the two parents who brought them into this world. The foundational human rights document in the world today regarding chil-

Former Pennsylvania Senator Rick Santorum on Gay Marriage

Same-sex marriage is completely deconstructing marriage and taking away a privilege that is given to two people, a man and a woman who are married, who have a child or adopt a child. We know it's best for children and for society that men and women get married. We know it's healthier. We know it's better for men. We know it's better for women. We know it's better for communities.

What we don't know is what happens with other options. And once you get away from the model of "what we know is best" and you get into the other options, from my perspective, there's no stopping it. And also from my perspective, you devalue what you want to value, which is a man and woman in marriage with a child or children. And when you devalue that, you get less of it. When you get less of it, society as a whole suffers.

Rick Santorum,
Pew Forum Interview, April 24, 2008.
http://pewforum.org.

dren, the 1989 U.N. Convention on the Rights of the Child, specifically guarantees children this right. The last time I checked, liberals like me were supposed to be in favor of internationally recognized human rights, particularly concerning children, who are typically society's most voiceless and vulnerable group. Or have I now said something I shouldn't?

Every child being raised by gay or lesbian couples will be denied his birthright to both parents who made him. Every single one. Moreover, losing that right will not be a consequence of something that at least most of us view as tragic, such as a marriage that didn't last, or an unexpected pregnancy where the father-to-be has no intention of sticking around. On the contrary, in the case of same-sex marriage and the children of those unions, it will be explained to everyone, including the children, that something wonderful has happened!

For me, what we are encouraged or permitted to say, or not say, to one another about what our society owes its children is crucially important in the debate over initiatives like California's Proposition 8, which would reinstate marriage's customary man-woman form. Do you think that every child deserves his mother and father, with adoption available for those children whose natural parents cannot care for them? Do you suspect that fathers and mothers are different from one another? Do you imagine that biological ties matter to children? How many parents per child is best? Do you think that "two" is a better answer than one, three, four or whatever? If you do, be careful. In making the case for same-sex marriage, more than a few grown-ups will be quite willing to question your integrity and goodwill. Children, of course, are rarely consulted.

Choosing One Good over Another

The liberal philosopher Isaiah Berlin famously argued that, in many cases, the real conflict we face is not good versus bad but good versus good. Reducing homophobia is good. Protecting the birthright of the child is good. How should we reason together as a society when these two good things conflict?

Here is my reasoning. I reject homophobia and believe in the equal dignity of gay and lesbian love. Because I also believe with all my heart in the right of the child to the mother and father who made her, I believe that we as a society should seek to maintain and to strengthen the only human institution—marriage—that is specifically intended to safeguard that right and make it real for our children.

Legalized same-sex marriage almost certainly benefits those same-sex couples who choose to marry, as well as the children being raised in those homes. But changing the meaning of marriage to accommodate homosexual orientation further and perhaps definitively undermines for all of us the very thing—the gift, the birthright—that is marriage's most distinctive contribution to human society. That's a change that, in the final analysis, I cannot support.

> *"Reparations present an opportunity to reconstruct Black civil discourse along more democratic lines."*

Slavery Reparations Would Promote Social Justice for African Americans

Clarence Lang

Clarence Lang argues in the following viewpoint that the U.S. government should grant financial reparations to African Americans as recompense for decades of slavery and second-class citizenship. Lang contends that reparations would help reinvigorate the black community by financing parks, medical services, and other social works. He believes African Americans would rally to their communities' aid and devise appropriate ways of disbursing the payments so that all would benefit. And while this project would certainly generate more—and much needed—activism among blacks, the reparation movement could also become part of a larger global movement against oppression, inspiring dialogue between African Americans and other victimized people across the world. Clarence Lang is an assistant professor of Afri-

Clarence Lang, "Reparations as a New Reconstruction," *Against the Current*, January–February 2003. Reproduced by permission.

can American studies and history at the University of Illinois in Urbana-Champaign. He has written several articles for the Journal of Social History, Race and Society *and other scholarly journals.*

As you read, consider the following questions:

1. How has the liberal leadership in the government forsaken the black community, according to Lang?

2. How does the author conceive of reparations as a Marshall Plan for urban areas?

3. As Lang notes, in what public and private arenas do the "crimes" of white privilege persist in America?

"The oppression of racism is a palpable part of life in America, so much so that the broader problems facing us today might have their solution in understanding the opposition that African Americans have put up against the system that has kept us down."

—Walter Mosley, Workin' on the Chain Gang: Shaking Off the Dead Hand of History *(2000)*

"Unreal" is the only way to begin to describe the period since November 2000. Economic recession, the continuing evisceration of the social safety net through the populist rhetoric of "cutting taxes" (for the wealthy), corporate deregulation, and federal marriage promotion schemes are all ominous signs.

Shrill American patriotism and militarism, naked animosity toward peoples of color, an authoritarian and secretive presidential administration, attempts at establishing a government informant program, and brazen attacks on political citizenship, civil liberties and labor rights—these developments are the distinctive features of American-style "Homeland Security."

The Democratic Party's capitulation to the George W. Bush presidency's pro-war, anti-labor and socially austere agenda ensures this new ascendancy. Yet every crisis creates opportunity: The present historical moment presents progressive communities with the chance not only to fight to derail the war machine and restore basic bourgeois freedoms, but also the opening to argue for visions that reflect our most radical imaginations.

Some envision a Green–Labor party merger, while others imagine a thorough reorientation of American foreign policy. The Black Liberation Movement similarly points in emancipatory directions: Resurgent mass sentiment and activity around the demand for reparations is a potentially powerful component of the broader fight for an equitable domestic and global order.

Retreat from Equality

It is fitting that an issue like reparations, involving African Americans, contains such possibilities.

In the first place, the present economic state of national emergency was manifest among African Americans during the supposed prosperity of the William Jefferson Clinton years, and only now has become more generalized. Moreover, the current hegemony of the Republican Party is a long-term consequence of a retreat from Black racial equality.

The fact that the Bush administration has gutted civil freedoms through executive action and laws like the USA PATRIOT Act should come as no surprise, considering Bush's "election" was in fact a legalistic coup, one accomplished through Black voter disfranchisement and harassment, and a Supreme Court perversion of a Constitutional amendment originally enacted to protect Black citizenship.

Practices of racially profiling African Americans in the "War on Drugs" established a precedent for the profiling and undue detainment of countless people of Arab descent, and Muslims. The militarization of space in many Black com-

The Civil Rights Struggle set the terms of political discourse for the 1960s, and had a transformative impact on an entire generation of activists. Even Black Power, much maligned as racial "separatism," expressed a fundamental desire for social justice; it drew from anticolonial movements abroad, and inspired other nationally oppressed peoples in the United States, as well as the antiwar and women's movement.

Reparations as Redistribution

Likewise, the contemporary call for reparations is much more than a crude attempt at extorting "money" for individuals, as critics on the right have dismissed. Neither does it constitute narrow, divisive "identity politics," as some on the left would have it.

The reparations demand reflects the powerful appeal of Black nationalism among African Americans, yet it is at root a social democratic demand with bases in international law and historical precedent. It also has groundings in the legacies of slavery, segregation, criminal urban neglect, and other private and state policies that have promoted the vast disparities of wealth between Black and white Americans.

Many Black people across class, ideological and political lines support it; but as with other Black democratic struggles, people across racial and national-ethnic lines would stand to gain, too.

For instance, massive reconstruction of inner city schools, neighborhoods and infrastructure, and full Black employment at livable wages, would also make many cities more habitable places, and improve the quality of life of all residents. Conceived as a domestic Marshall Plan for urban Black America, reparations would not just enrich African Americans by supplanting prisons, police, low wages and corporate tax abatements with a genuine social policy.

Redistributional policies targeted to African Americans could affect the structure of opportunities for working-class and poor people generally. On another plane, the reparations dialogue exposes for everyone the real sources of private wealth in the United States: the exploitation by the few of the labor and resources of the many.

Confronting Racial Injustices

As well, reparations places in stark relief the unearned privileges of whiteness aided and abetted by the federal government. These crimes persist in home ownership, employment, education, farm supports, health care, insurance rates, lending practices, the criminal justice system, access to public amenities, representation in public office and media, not to mention the location of environmental hazards that cause cancer and respiratory illness.

Besides serving this vital educational function, the present momentum behind reparations contains the germ of a politically reenergized and robust Black civil society, one connected to a movement culture of participatory democracy and collective leadership.

Scholars have criticized the elite brokerage model that has become dominant in contemporary Black politics. Political scientist Adolph L. Reed, Jr., in particular, has argued this model prevents mass participation in the shaping of agendas, and positions Black professionals and entrepreneurs as custodians who negotiate with white elites on behalf of organically derived, undifferentiated African American interests.

Reparations present an opportunity to reconstruct Black civil discourse along more democratic lines, though the fulfillment of this goal depends on Black radicals' creative energies in formulating a mass organizing strategy that goes beyond the provinces of a few skilled lawyers, politicians, would-be entrepreneurs, and Washington, D.C. politicos.

One approach might involve local community research projects representing a cross-section of Black America, including schoolteachers, youth, professional scholars and graduate students, nurses, janitors, health care and manufacturing workers, and community organizers.

These projects would be charged with collecting historical and recent data in individual cities about racial-class disparities in job markets, quality of housing, child welfare, the courts, police violence, elder care, and the land-use policies that have displaced or exploited Black communities.

Research could also highlight the local parks, schools, hospitals and other public institutions Black citizens supported for decades through their taxes, even as they were barred from using them through Jim Crow ordinances and state laws. Presenting this information at churches, labor halls, schools, and other open forums could make the case for reparations more concrete and close, and draw new activists into the struggle.

As a complement, local community councils could coordinate city-wide, door-to-door surveys in Black neighborhoods that gauge the actual depth of support for reparations, and get to the essence of how people would want reparations to look programmatically.

Fully funded home ownership, financed by the federal government and banking institutions that systematically denied Black people loans? Tuition and fee waivers at all state universities and colleges, and private schools that benefited from slavery and "negro removal" from choice properties?

Guaranteed employment at living wages? Land? Capital for launching cooperatively owned businesses, including multimedia outlets? Worker-run manufacturing? Free health care and state-of-the-art procedures, especially for those suffering the effects of HIV, drug dependency, and exposure to environmental pollutants?

Building Grassroots Power

Community-level canvassing could answer such inquiries, and at the same time lay the groundwork for confronting more far-reaching questions critical to our development over the long haul. How can African American communities ensure representativeness in local reparations projects, given the class-stratified character of Black America?

How would advocates reach a working accord around specific reparations proposals, strategies and tactics? What inclusive, democratic decision-making processes would this entail? How would we develop and promote new leadership? What role would anti-racist whites and other people of color play in a Black reparations movement?

What would be the role of musicians, poets, playwrights and other cultural workers, and what methods would they use to attract new audiences? Were reparations achieved, how would these resources be managed, and by whom, and how would we safeguard transparency in these procedures? What models of organization would we look to?

Without a popular approach, the Black petty bourgeoisie have carte blanche to build a reparations consensus embodying their own class-based interests, much as a nascent professional and business elite co-opted "Black Power" in the late '60s and early '70s.

The necessary spadework of mass organizing would allow Black progressive movement communities to learn collaboratively with, and from, our people, and cultivate solid constituencies for our programs on the ground.

As in previous moments of Black insurgency, we might offer new concepts of citizenship, social responsibility, and popular engagement in the making of public policies that value people over private profit.

An International Movement

As suggested by the 2001 World Conference Against Racism, reparations can become part of a much larger anti-globalist campaign involving the struggles of the Palestinian and Puerto Rican people, Mexican braceros, landless workers in the former settler colonies of southern Africa, Asian-American communities confronting hate crime violence, and citizens dealing with the effects of Structural Adjustment in developing nations.

In the process of responding to Black national oppression, we might also build closer solidarity with other working-class energies in the United States, including efforts toward a national health care system and a living wage amendment to the U.S. Constitution, and the end of company outsourcing to cheaper labor markets abroad.

In the short term, a reparations campaign might not achieve all that Black people are after. But we would feel our collective strength, empowered by asserting an agency and purpose that the Black Liberation Movement currently appears to lack.

Many of us, born in the post-Civil Rights/Black Power period, would for the first time find meaning in something transcendent of our individual selves. In the current climate of war, corporate pillaging, and repression, that would be a good enough start.

"There needs to be a series of tangible amends (reimbursements) to the Native Americans for past wrongs."

Restitution and Reparations Would Promote Social Justice for Native Americans

Joe Schriner

A former journalist, Joe Schriner has run for president of the United States since 2000 as an independent candidate. In the viewpoint that follows, Schriner describes what he would do for Native Americans if he were elected. Schriner believes that Native Americans deserve an apology and financial reparations for past wrongs done to the nation's tribes. He advocates the government's returning some stolen land, disbursing cash, and preserving reservation land from being exploited by business or government interests. These actions, he hopes, will atone for what he believes was the systematic genocide of the Native American people perpetrated by the government since the founding of the country.

Joe Schriner, "Native American Position Paper," Average Joe Schriner for President, 2008. Reproduced by permission of the author.

As you read, consider the following questions:

1. How does Schriner propose grade school, high school, and college curricula be altered as part of his reparation plan?

2. What lands does the author specifically say would be returned to Native Americans under his administration?

3. According to Schriner, how much money would his administration disburse to each Native American as restitution?

Something happened at the inception of our nation that pointed us in the wrong direction. And we're *still* going in the wrong direction with Native American affairs.

What's more, it's a blot on the collective American culture that has never really been reconciled. And we've never really made adequate amends for it either.

What hasn't been reconciled is the following:

In Camden, Maine, Fr. Eugene Gaffey, who worked at the St. Francis Apache River Reservation in Arizona, offered this take on history:

"For 2,000 years God creatively inspired many parts of the Native American culture, as God inspired many parts of the European culture," said Fr. Gaffey. In 1492, God began to orchestrate a "coming together" to create a wonderfully improved society, mixing the best of both cultures.

What happened instead was "perhaps the biggest incidence of genocide in the world," Native American activist Bruce Two Eagles was quoted in an edition of the *Mountain Xpress* newspaper. The article noted that in 1492, there was an estimated 20 million Native Americans. The 1890 U.S. Census showed only 250,000 Native Americans.

We'd picked up the *Mountain Xpress* on a campaign stop in North Carolina. On our next stop in North Augusta, South

Carolina, Tina Grover (a half-blood Native American) said to us that it wasn't just physical genocide—it was "cultural genocide."

In the process, land was taken by force or swindled by deceitful treaties.

Native American children were taken from their parents, put in boarding schools, forced to cut their hair, abandon their language and culture, so they could be "civilized."

And Ms. Grover added that the white man didn't just take Native American children, lives, land . . . "The white man took the Native American's spirit," she lamented.

How this translated, Harrison Jim of the Eagle Plume Society in Gallup, New Mexico, told us on a stop there, was that many Native Americans are still today experiencing the effects of "Post Colonial Stress Syndrome." (Same psychological features as Post Traumatic Stress Syndrome.)

And this affliction has passed from generation to generation, resulting in high incidence of poverty, alcoholism, domestic violence, suicide . . .

Apologizing for Past Wrongs

As president, at the outset I would go to a Reservation(s) and offer a heartfelt apology to the Native Americans for all the past atrocities committed by our forefathers and perpetuated, in part, by racist tendencies even until today.

Then to start heading in the direction we should have been going since the beginning, I believe that there needs to be a nationwide "Native American Renaissance."

We should start by creating a "Native American Awareness Division" within the Bureau of Indian Affairs expressly to design and institute a multi-dimensional plan for getting the uncensored, Native American message and story to the general populace in a broad-brush fashion.

The Division should include things like: a Native American Speaker's Bureau; a documentary production arm; the generation of more Native American literature; Native American theatre troupes ... (In Cortez, Colorado, I took our children to the *Black Shawl Drama*. Sponsored by the Cortez Cultural Center, it was a poignant re-enactment of the tragic, early days of our country as seen through Native American eyes.)

Revising History Lessons

In tandem with this push, I would also appoint a Native American Commission to help revise history books to better reflect Native American cultures, tribal dynamics and offer a closer (and much more expanded) look at the atrocities to Native Americans, not only at the beginning of this country, but throughout our history.

"The cost in human life (to the Native Americans) can't be accurately measured. And the suffering not even roughly measured," wrote Howard Zinn in his book *A Peoples' History of the United States*. "Most of the history books given to children pass quickly over it."

On a campaign stop in Florence, Alabama—along the Trail of Tears [path of Native American relocation in the nineteenth century]—a newspaper reporter said to us that history often gets skewed "because the victors always write the history books."

I would also propose that grade school and high school curriculum include classes specifically about Native Americans, and when possible, they be taught by Native Americans.

On a campaign stop in Wyoming, I learned that school trustees in Ranchester, Wyoming, approved a class on American Indian culture and hired an instructor from the nearby Crow Reservation to teach it.

Besides existing Native American classes at a collegiate level, we would propose actual minors, and majors, in Native American Studies. And we would propose the Federal Government provide grants to get such programs going.

In Missoula, Montana, Chris Landis told us that she had taken college courses on Native American culture and has a personal quest of helping to save as much of the culture as possible. She also said she wanted to incorporate as much of the culture and spiritual practices into her own personal life, while still maintaining her Catholicism.

In Carmel Valley, California, I met with Fr. Scott McCarthy, a Catholic priest who has spent a considerable amount of time on Native American Reservations around the country and wrote the book *Earth Centered Theology*. The book explains how Fr. McCarthy draws from Native American rituals in practicing his Catholic faith. (For instance during some Masses, Fr. McCarthy burns sage on the altar and says the Our Father in the Lakota Tribe's language.)

It is in these types of pursuits (as with studying the Native American environmental stewardship model, the intricacies of their tribal village orientation, family and ancestral traditions . . .), that we will learn what we should have learned from the beginning.

And while it will take generations to meld the cultures, we will—at last—collectively be going in the right direction.

Note: And this is if the Native Americans even *want* to move toward a melding of cultures. This would need to be explored at an in-depth level at the outset.

Returning Land to the Tribes

To continue in the 'right direction,' there needs to be a series of tangible amends (reimbursements) to the Native Americans for past wrongs.

We took much of their land through unadulterated greed. We consistently killed the Native Americans, drove others from the land (like in the Trail of Tears), or took the land through broken treaties and other deceits.

I met with Teton Tribe member Richard Shangreaux in a tipi in Pierre, South Dakota. He told me amends should encompass making right the treaties and returning some of the land.

As an example, he said the Black Hills of South Dakota were an incredibly "sacred place" to the Native Americans. But once gold was discovered there, the U.S. Government took the land from the Native Americans.

Our administration would propose giving it back. And our administration would propose giving, for instance, a percentage of some of the National Forests to the Native Americans.

And while the tribes in the South Dakota area look at the Black Hills as sacred, the Dine Tribe in Hoteville, Arizona, look at their land as sacred as well. However, the Dine's Tom Bedonie had been traveling the country trying to raise awareness that the Dine land was in jeopardy. I heard him talk in Columbia, Missouri, where he said energy companies interested in extracting coal from that area of Arizona were creating pressure for the relocation of 10,000 Dine Tribe members.

This simply harkens back to the forced Native American relocations of old, for material gain. As president, I would push for a moratorium on any more Native American relocations.

Preserving Reservations

And while logistically it would be difficult to return all the land, a series of creative initiatives could be undertaken to come at this in a variety of ways.

For instance, the Federal Government (in tandem with private citizen fundraising) could help fund the White Earth Land Preservation Project, and similar projects on Reservations across the country.

On a campaign stop at White Earth Reservation in northern Minnesota, we talked with White Earth Preservation Project Director Winnona La Duke. (Ms. La Duke, an Ojibwe

Joel Pett Editorial Cartoon, used with the permission of Joel Pett and the Cartoonist Group. All rights reserved.

Tribe member, ran as [independent candidate] Ralph Nader's vice-presidential candidate during Campaign 2000.)

We learned the project had established a fund to buy back Reservation property sold to such concerns as corporate farms. On this land, they were replanting indigenous trees, reintroducing sturgeon to the area rivers, teaching the Native Americans the ways of ancestral organic farming, traditional hunting, and so on.

Ms. La Duke said the Ojibwe's ethos is to respect the earth and live as if one is responsible for "the next seven generations."

Another way to give back some of the land would be to get behind an initiative of the Nez Perz Tribe living along the Columbia River in Idaho.

At Findlay College in Ohio, we heard the Nez Perz's Allen Pinkham say that, for generations, his people relied heavily on Columbia River salmon runs. But as more and more people moved to the Pacific Northwest, there was a greater demand for electrical power. So the Columbia River was tapped for power with a series of hydroelectric dams—that all but ended the salmon runs.

Pinkham said his tribe was trying to get some of the dams in the area removed and was asking people to "shut off one light for one salmon." That is, Pinkham's tribe is asking people in the Northwest to cut back on their energy use in general to decrease the need for as many dams.

We would shut off more than one light (cut back the thermostat, stop using air conditioning, put up a wind turbine . . .) in the White House for this—not to mention to reverse global warming. And we would give some of the money to the Nez Perz's Chief Joseph Foundation, which our family personally has already done.

Cash Reparations

A famous quote by the Nez Perz's Chief Joseph summed up the Native American plight of the past: ". . . The old men are all dead. The little children are freezing to death. My people—some of them have run away to the hills and have no blankets, no food . . . I want to have time to look for my children . . . I will fight no more forever."

Then to make even more amends, our administration would propose every Native American, trans-generational war victim—and that would be *every* Native American—would receive $25,000 in reparations. (The U.S. government has recently awarded every Japanese WWII internment camp prisoner $20,000 in reparations.)

And because of the trans-generational nature of Post Colonial Stress Syndrome, many of these Native Americans have been mental and emotional 'prisoners' as well.

At a seminar on Racism that I attended at Ohio's Bluffton College, it was explained that colonialism is: "An act of aggression against a people by a country which takes land, exploits resources (including the indigenous people of the land), destroys indigenous culture and requires allegiance to the conquering country."

Drug and Alcohol Counseling

Post Colonial Stress Syndrome has, in part, led to transgenerational alcoholism in some of the Native American people.

In Gallup, New Mexico, the Navahos Gabe Kanawite is trying to do something about this. Out of a sense of personal responsibility and grief about what is happening to his people, Kanawite told me he shifted his college major from accounting to drug and alcohol counseling.

Likewise on the Osage Reservation in Oklahoma, Osage Tribe member Monte Roubideaux told me he was at nearby Bacon College majoring in drug and alcohol counseling as well. "I want to give back to my people," he said.

As part of reparations, our administration would propose providing more college grants to Native Americans like Kanawite and Roubideaux for pursuing this type of major. What's more, our administration would propose more funding for such Reservation Drug and Alcohol Treatment Centers as the Eagle Plume Society Center (mentioned earlier) in Gallup.

Native American Cultural Education

The Eagle Plume Society not only helps Native Americans get clean and sober, it helps them "Get Navaho!" On a tour of the center, Harrison Jim told us he tries to help the Navaho recover from Post Traumatic Colonial Stress Syndrome through "talking circles" to deal, not only with their addiction, but also the trauma of western philosophy encroachment. These Navahos are encouraged to reconnect with their native roots, sacred songs, sacred prayers, age-old ceremonies . . . (Our administration would propose financial help for more treatment models like the Eagle Plume Society.)

Osage Monte Roubideaux is also trying to learn as much about his tribe's culture, including learning the language. And he is now teaching it to his children as well.

In Pawhuska, Oklahoma (also on the Osage Indian Reservation), Stephanie Mashunkashey told me she would like to see the Federal Government help subsidize more Native American cultural education for all tribal youth, and adults— because of the cultural genocide that was committed against her people, leading many to be quite out of touch with their roots. (Our administration would agree, and push for more funding help in this area as well.). . .

A Yearly Memorial

As we followed the 1,200 mile Trail of Tears on a research trip, we learned gold had been discovered in south Georgia, and shortly after the Georgia legislature declared Cherokee land confiscated, opening the door to the forced march— through the winter—to Oklahoma.

Men were seized from their fields, women from their spinning wheels and children from their play. Some 4,000 of these men, women and children (almost one-fourth) died along the way, according to literature about the Trail.

"It was the cruelest work I ever knew," said one U.S. militiaman.

Congress has designated some of the main routes west as the Trail of Tears National Historic Trail.

Our administration would go much further.

We would call for a week of national mourning for, not only the Trail of Tears deaths, but *all* the Native American deaths at U.S. hands. These would be days filled with graphic eulogies about these things, town education forums, TV specials, marches . . .

And as a follow-up, we would propose a yearly "Native American National History Month" every year.

"I have no apologies to make to people I have not offended. If offenses were committed they weren't my fault, or for that matter yours or that of any living Americans."

African Americans and Native Americans Do Not Deserve Reparations

Michael Reagan

Mike Reagan, the eldest son of former President Ronald Reagan, is a conservative radio show commentator on the Radio America Network. In the following viewpoint, Reagan argues that African Americans and Native Americans do not deserve reparations for the treatment of their ancestors. In Reagan's view, living Americans cannot atone for sins they did not commit. He also believes that if reparations are considered, then it would not be difficult for immigrant groups and other mistreated segments of the population to clamor for their share of the payback.

As you read, consider the following questions:

1. According to Reagan, in what way were the reparations to black slaves already paid?

Michael Reagan, "Where Are My Reparations?" FrontPageMag.com, August 4, 2008. Reproduced by permission.

2. In the author's opinion, how were his ancestors the victims of abuse in America?

3. How are millions of Americans already making reparations to Native Americans, in Reagan's opinion?

L ike altar boys who used to strike their breasts and mutter "mea culpa" ("through my fault") during the beginning of the Latin mass while confessing that they had sinned, Democrats are in full confessional mode, apologizing for every real or imagined sin against a particular group they believe their country once offended.

In the latest example of sheer looniness that has marked the current Democrat-controlled Congress, surely the worst if not the craziest Congress in all U.S. history, the House officially sought forgiveness from Native Americans and the victims of Jim Crow-ism.

They did that in our name, laying upon our shoulders the sins of long-dead Americans and having us cringe at the feet of today's casino-rich Native Americans, and our black brothers and sisters whose votes they lust after.

Atoning Now for Past Sins

Just a minute here. Neither I nor any of my immediate ancestors ever lifted a finger against a single American Indian or black American. I have no apologies to make to people I have not offended. If offenses were committed they weren't my fault, or for that matter yours or that of any living Americans.

How dare these congressional demagogues associate us with alleged sins of the distant past committed by people who have long been gone from this world.

Then there are the people who think that we should pay reparations to the descendants of slaves, or bow and scrape before the offspring of long-dead Native Americans for having

Who Should Get Reparation?

The current reparations movement overlooks many important facts. First, reparations usually are paid to direct victims. The U.S. Government apologized and paid compensation to Japanese-Americans interned during World War II, and Holocaust survivors received payments from Germany. In addition, not all blacks were slaves, and an estimated 3,000 blacks were slaveholders. Many immigrants not only came to the U.S. long after slavery ended, but many of them were also confronted with discrimination. Should they pay reparations, too? Or should they receive them?

Allan C. Brownfeld, Right Side News,
July 9, 2009. www.rightsidenews.com.

maltreated their ancestors who themselves were not lax in maltreating paleface settlers who they tended to scalp when the opportunity arose.

They say we owe black folks for slavery and Jim Crow laws, forgetting that the debt was fully paid by the 360,000 Union soldiers who died in the Civil War to free the ancestors of today's black Americans. The debt was marked "paid in full," written in their blood.

I'm sure that one of my ancestors offended somebody or other at one time. Am I expected to reimburse their present-day offspring if any happen to show up for a handout?

Immigrants Also Mistreated

And, by the way, if we are going to pay reparations to the descendants of any group who was grievously mistreated, sign me up. I'm Irish, and no group of immigrants was more badly treated.

Poor, hungry and impoverished, they arrived on these shores where they were welcomed by help-wanted signs proclaiming, "No Irish need apply." The *New York Times* of the day was full of ads reading "Wanted, coachmen. Must be sober, industrious and reliable. No Irish need apply."

Not that there were many Irishmen available to be coachmen because vast numbers of them, many brand new arrivals here, were elsewhere, fighting and dying at places like Gettysburg and Antietam so that the native born dandies in New York who wouldn't fight for their country would be safe at home and able to hire coachmen or mistreat their Irish chambermaids.

It took years for the wave of Irish emigrants fleeing from harsh British rule and a famine that killed an estimated million-and-a-half of them before it was over to lift themselves out of grinding poverty. And they did it on their own, without any help.

Where are my reparations?

More Pressing Concerns

As for making reparations to Native Americans, millions of our fellow citizens are doing that already, filling the swollen coffers of the host of gambling casinos thriving on Indian reservations. Long-gone Americans drove them off their ancestral lands. Today's Americans are paying for it at their roulette tables or playing slot machines.

If there is any apologizing to be done, the Democrats in Congress should be doing it, atoning for $4-a-gallon gas that's the direct result of their refusal to allow us to tap the billions if not trillions of gallons of oil lying untapped here, in Alaska and in the Gulf, because they won't let us go after them and free ourselves from dependence on foreign oil.

If they want to chant "mea culpa," let the guilt-ridden Democrats pay us reparations out of their campaign war-chest for getting us into this mess.

Periodical Bibliography

The following articles have been selected to supplement the diverse views presented in this chapter.

Thomas Craemer	"Framing Reparations," *Policy Studies Journal*, 2009.
John Aloysius Farrell	"Obama's Election Shows That Affirmative Action's Day Has Passed," *U.S. News & World Report*, June 10, 2009.
Mark Galli	"Is the Gay Marriage Debate Over?" *Christianity Today*, July 2009.
Robert P. George	"Gay Marriage, Democracy, and the Courts," *Wall Street Journal*, August 3, 2009.
Dana Goldstein	"Reparations Anxiety," *American Prospect*, January/February 2008.
Investor's Business Daily	"Discrimination: The Issue That Won't Go Away," July 2, 2009.
Lisa Miller	"Our Mutual Joy," *Newsweek*, December 15, 2008.
Martha Nussbaum	"A Right to Marry?" *Dissent*, Summer 2009.
Jeffrey Rosen	"Race to the Top," *New Republic*, May 6, 2009.
Stuart Taylor	"Sotomayor, Gates and Race," *National Journal*, August 1, 2009.

CHAPTER 3

What Policies Would Promote Social Justice for Women?

Chapter Preface

In a March 1986 *Wall Street Journal* article, journalists Carol Hymowitz and Timothy D. Schellhardt used the term "glass ceiling" to describe an invisible barrier that prevented women from attaining higher-paying leadership positions in the business world. While not the first time it was used to describe the difficulty women face in achieving promotions, the article popularized the term and raised public awareness about gender inequality in the work place—especially at the highest levels. Since the publication of the article, social justice for women in business, politics, education, and other areas has been closely studied. Arguably, much progress has been made, and women currently hold leadership positions in many Fortune 500 companies in a wide range of industries; however, in the majority of the companies, men still occupy the highest levels of leadership.

Gender discrimination is not limited to the business world. There have been many reports of women encountering a glass ceiling in academic settings as well. The existence of gender bias within higher education gained national attention in 2005 when then-president of Harvard University, Lawrence H. Summers, speaking at a conference, provided three possible reasons as to why women were underrepresented in science and engineering fields. Two of the possibilities that Summers touched on are fairly well accepted in sociological circles: (1) women often desire to focus on family instead of work and (2) the continuing presence of discrimination in academia. Summers' third reason, however, generated controversy. He hypothesized that the small number of women in scientific fields could be explained by "the different availability of aptitude at the high end"; in other words, an innate difference between the capabilities of men and women.

Many women reacted strongly to Summers' comments, calling them sexist and indicative of gender bias. Massachusetts Institute of Technology biology professor Nancy Hopkins attended the conference where Summers was speaking, then walked out during his speech and contacted the press about the remarks. At the center of much of the media coverage of the controversy, Hopkins remained hopeful that the public's awareness would be raised on the prejudice that women scientists and mathematicians face. She stated, "People will realize what these women face. They must deal with men like Larry Summers. . . . They'll tell you they have no bias, but in their head they are thinking, 'Can women really do math?'" Hopkins's statements echoed the sentiments of many women scientists—gender discrimination restricts achievement in the academic sphere.

While the reaction of most women to the controversial speech was outrage, some women were critical of the indignant responses. Journalist Sally Quinn wrote in the *Washington Post* that "some of the women who heard what Larry Summers said did exactly what they are stereotypically criticized for doing. They got hysterical." Quinn does not claim to know whether men and women possess different aptitudes at science and math; however, she insists that there are innate differences between men and women, and ability in math and science might be among those differences.

Examining the reasons why women are underrepresented in leadership positions and math and science fields is only one aspect in assuring the achievement of social justice for women. The viewpoints in the following chapter assess how much progress has been made in securing equality for women in business, politics, and sports. Additionally, the authors of these viewpoints examine what policies would best foster a continued reduction of gender bias in these aspects of society.

> "Even though progress has been considerable over the last few decades, at the current speed of change it would still take 50 years for women to close the pay gap."

The Gender Wage Gap Needs to Be Remedied

Ashley English and Ariane Hegewisch

The gender wage gap refers to the difference in earnings between men and women in the workplace, with women's jobs typically paying less than men's requiring a similar skill level. In the following viewpoint, Ashley English and Ariane Hegewisch reveal the findings of a report analyzing fifteen years of data on men's and women's salaries which, they conclude, confirms a gender wage gap does exist. English and Hegewisch argue that while advances have been made in closing the wage gap between the genders, new policies are necessary to ensure that the recently stagnating progress does not cease completely. Ashley English is a special assistant to Heidi Hartmann, president of the Institute for Women's Policy Research (IWPR), and Ariane Hegewisch, study director at the IWPR, is charged with conducting and overseeing research on gender discrimination in the workplace.

Ashley English and Ariane Hegewisch, "Still a Man's Labor Market: The Long-Term Earnings Gap," *Research-in-Brief #C366*, February 2008. Reproduced by permission.

As you read, consider the following questions:

1. According to the report cited by English and Hegewisch, how much did women earn compared with men and what is the gap between the earnings over the 15 year period under examination?

2. What reasons do the authors give to explain why men's and women's earnings differ?

3. What are some of the policy suggestions laid out by the authors to combat the gender wage gap?

Many argue that women's prospects in the labor market have steadily increased and that any small remaining gap in earnings between women and men is not significant. They see the remaining differences as the result of women's own choices, or they argue that with women now graduating from college at a higher rate than men, and with the economy continuing its shift toward services, work and earnings differences between women and men may disappear entirely.

Evidence of Wage Gap

It is true that women have made progress relative to men. Women's labor force participation has risen rapidly; women have made progress in many occupations that previously were bastions of men; the wage gap has narrowed by more than one-third since 1960, from women earning 59 cents for every dollar earned by men, to 77 cents now. Yet this measure, by virtue of including only those who worked full-time for at least 50 weeks per year, excludes almost half of all women. While women's and men's work and careers have become more similar, important differences remain. Women are much more likely than men to reduce or interrupt their time in paid work to deal with family responsibilities, resulting in a dramatic impact on their earnings. Over a 15-year period [from 1983 to 1998] less than half of all women (48.5 percent) had earnings in each of the 15 years, compared with 6 of 7 (84 percent) men; 3 of 10 women report four or more years without earnings (compared with 1 of 20 men). Women are also more likely to work fewer hours per year, working on average 500 hours fewer per year (or 22 percent less) than men, even when only men and women who have earnings in each year are compared.

This division of responsibility for family care results in very different wages and hours of work for men and women. Over the 15 years, the more likely a woman is to have dependent children and be married, the more likely she is to be a low earner and have fewer hours in the labor market. The opposite holds for men: marriage and dependent children make it much more likely that a man has higher earnings and works longer hours.

When actual earnings are accumulated over many years for all men and women workers, the losses to women and their families due to the wage gap are large and can be devastating. The average woman earned only $273,592 while the average man earned $722,693, leaving a gap of 62 percent over the 15-year period.

The report is based on an analysis of the Panel Study of Income Dynamics (PSID). The PSID is a longitudinal data set that tracks a representative sample of households over time. This analysis uses data from 1983 to 1998 and includes all prime-age workers (26 to 59 years old) who have at least one year of positive earnings during that period and who have provided information on labor market activity for each of the 15 years: 1,614 women and 1,212 men. All earnings have been converted into 1999 dollars.

Women's High Salaries Are Men's Low

The earnings gap is not simply explained by women having less time in paid work. Hour per hour, including only those women and men with the strongest labor market attachment who had earnings every single year, in this study women still earn only 69.6 cents of each dollar earned per hour by men.

Again including only those with the strongest labor force attachment, women are significantly more likely to have low earnings (less than $15,000 annually—just above the poverty line for a family of three in 1999) than men. One in three women had four or more years with earnings below this threshold, compared with one in fourteen men. Over the whole 15 years only a tiny minority of men (1.3 percent) fail to average at least $15,000 per year, compared with 17.7 percent of strongly attached women. Ninety percent of those who average less than $15,000 per year are women.

The average annual earnings for most men and most women (with earnings in each of 15 years) were in the range of $25,000 to $49,999. But for men, that is virtually the bottom of the salary range: 44.5 percent of men earned more than $50,000 annually. For women, it's the top; only 9.6 percent of women on average earned more than $50,000 per year.

However the wage gap is calculated, it is important to note that men's and women's earnings differ for many reasons including: discrimination in the labor market, discrimination in pre-labor market preparation (education/retiring programs), unequal societal norms at home, and the constrained decisions men and women make about work and home issues, which often result in women working fewer hours when they work and taking several years out of the labor market. . . . Many economists believe the 'remaining unexplained gap' can include the effects of discrimination.

Assessing Men's and Women's Jobs

Women also face a striking degree of sex segregation in the labor market—women work in predominantly 'women's jobs' and men in predominantly 'men's jobs,' that is, in jobs where the majority of workers are of one sex. To investigate this division and its impact on earnings further, the report divides jobs into three tiers or clusters—'elite' jobs, 'good' jobs, and 'less-skilled' jobs. Within each tier, occupations are classified as either male dominated or female dominated, thus resulting in six clusters. For both genders, approximately 58 percent of strongly attached workers, those with earnings in all 15 years, work consistently in a *single* one of the six career occupational clusters (spending at *least* 12 of 15 years in that cluster). The remaining 42 percent have mixed work histories, mainly rotating among jobs in the bottom two tiers. At least 75 percent of workers are of one gender within each of the six tiered gender clusters. Male and female pairs of occupations within each tier require an equivalent level of education and skills. The three male clusters account for half of all male workers; less than one in ten men (8 percent) work in the female dominated clusters; the remaining male workers had mixed work experience. Women are a little less likely to work in a cluster dominated by their own sex than men (44 percent) and more likely than men to work in a job where the majority of workers are of the other sex (15 percent)—not surprisingly, given that male dominated jobs traditionally pay more.

In each tier, women's jobs pay significantly less than their male counterparts. This is so even though both sets of occupations tend to require the same level of educational preparation; it also holds when only full-time workers (at least 1,750 hour—35 weeks for at least 50 weeks per year) are included.

Moreover, both men and women earn more in the male sector of each tier than their counterparts do in the female sector in the same tier; indicating a premium for working in male-typed jobs, and conversely, a penalty for working in female-typed jobs. (In the elite tier, women actually earn less per hour in male jobs than female jobs, yet their annual earnings are higher in the male jobs because women in men's jobs work more hours; despite slightly lower hourly earnings, their overall earnings opportunities may be better in the male sector.) Yet men tend to earn more than women in all tiers. In

Gender Gap in Youth Wages

Based on median annual earnings of dependent youths [collected by the Bureau of Labor Statistics in 1997], we observe approximately equal annual median earnings for both genders during their early employment years. Among the 12- to 13-year-olds, boys, on average, make $120, while girls make only slightly more, $125. If for no other reason this is important because it is the first instance of gender equality in earnings in the American labor force. As a further analysis shows, by the time that the youths in the study are in the second age group, 14- to 15-year-olds, boys' earnings surpass girls' wages substantially, with boys earning an average of $400 a year, and girls earning only $266. Thus, we observe the beginnings of the gender wage gap, and it only widens with older groups. Within the third group, 16- to 19-year-old boys, on average, make $950, while their female counterparts earn only $750.

Although comparing yearly wages is the conventional and more reliable method of measurement, the low hourly pay and relatively fewer hours worked at earlier ages makes it important to consider the hourly pay rate. Interestingly, parallel with the above findings, we observe that, for the 14- to 15-year-olds, boys have higher hourly wages than girls.

Yasemin Besen-Cassino,
NWSA Journal, *Spring 2008.*

the highest paid tier, male elite jobs, men on average earned $74,877 compared with $51,085 for full-time female workers (in 1999 dollars).

Men Work More Hours

Another striking difference between male and female dominated jobs is in the number of hours worked on average per year. Male dominated jobs, and jobs where neither sex is in a clear majority, have significantly more work hours per year than female dominated jobs at each level. This also holds for each gender—women in male dominated jobs on average work longer than women in female dominated jobs, and men in female dominated jobs work fewer hours on average than men in male dominated jobs. This suggests that the occupational difference in work hours goes beyond mere 'preference' by individual men and women and reflects a more systematic adjustment in hours to the gendered norm in the division of family labor.

The differences in average annual hours are partly a reflection of the greater likelihood for women to work reduced hours (less than 1,750 hours per year). Yet the differences are also stark when only those men and women working full-time are included (those who work at least 35 hours per week for 50 weeks per year). Men in elite male or elite female jobs typically work over an hour more per week than women in similar jobs. Men in 'good' female jobs on average work over three hours more per week than women in similar jobs. The pattern is less clear in the less skilled jobs.

Yet the difference in hours does not account for the earnings gap. Men outearn women hour by hour, even when only women with the strongest labor market attachment are included.

Women Have Experienced Wage Growth

One disadvantage of averaging male and female earnings data over the 15-year period is that such an average cannot show whether earnings disparities were higher at the beginning than at the end of the period. The earnings gap between women and men during the period from 1983 to 1998 was significantly smaller than for the previous 15-year period, a reflection of women spending fewer years out of the labor market and gaining more education and skills. To analyze whether the earnings gap has narrowed further during the period, the authors compute an average annual change rate in earnings for each worker (with at least two years of earnings). The analysis divides workers into three age groups at the start of the period, to check whether the pattern for younger women significantly differs from older women, and then estimates annual growth rates over the period for men and women. The normal assumption is that over time average earnings will increase as workers progress through their careers and gain seniority and skills, but earnings, of course, might also stall or decline.

The analysis shows significant gender differences, with men on average being less likely to have seen earnings growth over the period (58 percent of men compared to 73 percent of women) and more likely to have had an actual decline in earnings (26 percent of men compared to 19 percent of women). Younger men (those aged 26 to 31 in 1983) tended to do better than older men (39 to 45 years) but even in this age group one-third had no or negative earnings growth. Younger women also did better than older women, with "only" one-fifth of them having stable or decreasing earnings compared with 44 percent of women in the older cohort.

Some Women Outearn Husbands

This finding of stagnating or declining earnings for men over time corresponds to other studies. As the manufacturing sector struggled during the 1980s, many men experienced stagnating or falling earnings. Women's earnings rose both because they were in a better place in the labor market and because they increased their education and their labor market attachment. While the generally narrowing pay gap is encouraging, it is important to keep two caveats in mind: women started at such a low level that it was relatively easy to move up; and women with work interruptions likely had to start again at a much reduced level before they experienced large earning gains. Yet even though women are catching up, progress is slow and the pay gap continues to be substantial and unlikely to narrow much further without major policy adjustments.

While much of the data confirms that men generally earn more than women, this does not hold for all couples. Among the group of women who had earnings in each year, and were married for the whole period (about one-third of all women in the sample), 15 percent outearned their husbands (even if often the difference was not large). Hourly wages are higher than their husbands' for almost one-quarter of the women in this group (although, because hours might be lower, not all of them had higher average annual earnings). And, even though different working patterns mean that women earn less over the long term, among college educated women more than 85 percent had higher hourly earnings than their husbands in at least one year of the survey period.

Wage Gap Narrowing Has Stalled

Although women have made some gains relative to men, progress has stalled since the early 1990s. The gender gap in earnings has a major influence on families' life opportunities, on their likelihood of experiencing poverty, on older women's retirement security, and on single mothers' ability to provide for their children's care and education. Married women continue to be at least partially insulated from the impact of women's low earnings through their connection to higher earning men. Yet most families would have a higher standard of living if women's wages and lifetime earnings were higher. Single mothers, and their families, with no other household income to make up for the lower earnings available in most women's jobs, are particularly penalized. Furthermore, women's low life-time earnings can have devastating effects in old age by preventing women from building up sufficient resources for retirement. Widowed, divorced, or never married women over age 65 share high poverty rates of approximately 20 percent.

Gender Differences Self-Reproducing

Gender differentiation in the labor market is self-reproducing. When students express interest in non-traditional jobs, they are often not encouraged to pursue the appropriate career preparation by guidance counselors. Employers may pay women less because they believe women are more likely to leave work. They may structure jobs to provide part-time hours because they believe women are dependent on jobs with shorter work hours. Without subsidized child care, many families are left to their own resources to combine family care with paid work. When the husband outearns the wife, it makes greater economic sense for the wife, as the lower earner, to provide more or all of the child care because less income is lost if the lower-earner cuts back her work.

This gendered division of labor is self-reinforcing. Yet it is also arguably increasingly unstable and unsustainable. Men and women spend growing portions of their lives unmarried. Women's expectations are changing and they are demanding more independence and greater economic security throughout life, whether they are single or married. Women are closing the graduate school gap with men. Women have begun to outnumber men in law and medical schools and have increased their numbers substantially in business schools. But even though progress has been considerable over the last few decades, at the current speed of change it would still take 50 years for women to close the pay gap. Policy makers need to develop new policy interventions that can help break the vicious cycle that makes women trade down their progress at work and makes men lose out on family time.

Suggestions for Policies

There is not a single cause, and hence no single solution, that will deliver equality to men and women in the labor market. The factors contributing to the long-term pay gap include continued direct discrimination in the labor market; the undervaluation of work typically performed by women; the lack of systematic work family supports; the particular disadvantages faced by the growing number of women-headed households; the marriage penalties in the tax system; the underrepresentation of women in higher paying occupations; and poor working conditions in the labor market especially for lower skilled jobs. A program responding to these problems needs to include:

- Policies that reduce sex discrimination in the labor market: Providing more resources to oversight agencies including the Equal Employment Opportunity Commission and the Office of Federal Contract Compliance would strengthen the enforcement of equal opportunity laws and lead to resolving complaints more quickly. Developing new Equal Employment Opportunity remedies to address the comparable worth problem could require employers to show that comparable jobs are paid fairly, using tools such as job evaluation systems.

- Policies that make it easier to combine paid work with family work: Affordable, good quality early care and education for children has many benefits, including making it easier for lower income mothers to stay in the workforce. New policies are needed to make workplaces more family-friendly, including more flexible hours and job-guaranteed paid leaves for sickness and family care, the elimination or capping of mandatory overtime, a shorter standard work week, and the increased availability of better quality, reduced hours jobs. Last but not least, encouraging men to use family leave and reduce their work hours—and tackling discrimination faced by men who take up family leave or adjust hours to deal with family care—will help change the double-standard in parenting that places the responsibility for it on women.

- Education and training policies to increase women's presence in higher paying jobs: Increasing resources for non-traditional skills training, improving access to vocational training especially for single mothers, and improving career counseling and information available to girls and young women still in school are all important as there are still too many women who have been discouraged from pursuing higher education and/or job training for occupations that are not traditionally held by women.

- Policies to increase the support for women-headed households: Families headed by single mothers who face discrimination and lower earnings in the labor market are much more likely to live in poverty. Female-headed households need increased support in the forms of improved access to the income of non-custodial fathers after divorce, improved child care support, and improved access to vocational training and education programs designed to make it possible for single mothers to participate.

- Policies to reduce the "marriage penalty": Reducing the bias in income taxes and Social Security benefits on the secondary earner in a marriage will reduce the disincentives that depress the work effort of the lower earning member of a married couple.

- Policies to tackle the low-wage labor market: Policies that raise the minimum wage and provide resources for its proper enforcement and programs that encourage increased unionization will provide higher wages and increased access to benefits for low-wage workers, who are disproportionately female.

| *"The wage gap has been thoroughly de-
bunked and certified non-existent."*

The Gender Wage Gap
Is a Myth

Stephen Jarosek

*The difference between men's and women's earnings, termed the
gender wage gap, is commonly framed as a discrimination issue.
Stephen Jarosek, however, argues in the following viewpoint that
the wage gap is not an example of gender bias, but instead is
only the result of women making the choice not to work or to
work fewer hours. Jarosek contends that many women who ac-
quire high-level degrees in business, law, medicine, or other high-
paying fields often forsake further advancement in favor of pursuing family life. For this reason, women often do not put in the
time or effort to achieve the same pay that their male peers are
earning. Jarosek concludes that women and men simply make
different choices in the work world and that many men are more
willing to sacrifice personal time to commit to work while many
women are not. Stephen Jarosek is a systems theorist whose work
focuses on the study of the interaction of complex systems in na-*

Stephen Jarosek, "The Wage Gap Myth Is Hazardous to Men's Health," Mensnewsdaily
.com, July 7, 2005. Reproduced by permission of the author.

ture, science, and society. He is the author of the book Sanity's Insanity: Applying Semiotics to Understand the Hidden World of Mind, Culture and Gender Roles.

As you read, consider the following questions:

1. What is the "choices gap" described by the author?

2. What instances does Jarosek cite from the article by Lisa Belkin to show that women are making the choice not to work or are using an "escape hatch"?

3. According to Jarosek, which gender is running the world?

A study in the May issue of *American Economic Review* (2003) had found that the wage gap between men and women was the result of lifestyle choices, and not discrimination. It was found that choice, not discrimination, is the determining factor in wage difference 97 percent of the time. The wage gap myth has been debunked numerous times—for example, by the Independent Women's Forum, and the publication, "Women's Figures," by [economist Diana] Furchtgott-Roth and [feminist author Christine] Stolba.

The wage gap fiction was derived from the median wages of all men and all women in the work force, without regard to age, education, occupation, experience or working hours.

It's pretty obvious, isn't it? You'd think that if you had to explain something so self-explanatory, you might as well not bother and go and live in an ashram [village located away from human civilization to allow residents to focus on spirituality] in India.

A Choices, Not a Wage, Gap

We know how it goes. . . . Women are more likely to work fewer hours so that they can have more time to devote to the caring of children. Men are more likely to value career and therefore work longer hours per day, devoting many more years to developing their expertise that makes them more valuable. Men are more likely to work in the death careers, such as mining (and therefore get paid more), whereas women are more likely to work in air-conditioned offices, regardless of their skill-level. Women are more likely to pull out of careers in order to raise a family—the stay-at-home mom is a legitimate, fulfilling option and an ideal escape-hatch. No such fulfilling option is extended to men. The man who chooses the stay-at-home option becomes an invisible drone, of no interest to men or women, employers or government, God or country. And so on.

The various studies that have been coming out have been equalizing the wage-gap disparities, and so feminists no longer have any basis to claim discrimination on the basis of income.

As a further, very dramatic, example, there was the *New York Times* article by Lisa Belkin, "The Opt-Out Revolution," published on the 26th of October, 2003. After arraying a formidable and damning indictment of a revolution choosing to opt out instead of persisting with the good fight, Ms Belkin asks the rhetorical question, "Why don't women run the world?" Her answer is "Maybe it's because they don't want to."

Precisely. The wage gap is not a wage gap at all. It is a choices gap. Put simply, women have more choices than men. In most cases, their additional choices (e.g., stay-at-home-mom) require men to continue providing for them, and this is the reason for the wages gap.

Women Choose Not to Work

Let's take a closer look at some of Ms Belkin's observations.

- Stanford class of 1981—57% of mothers spent at least a year at home caring for their infant children in the first decade after graduation. One out of four have stayed home three or more years.

- Harvard Business School—In a survey of women from the classes of 1981, 1985 and 1991 it was found that only 38% were working full time.

- In surveys of professional women across the board— Between one quarter and one third are out of the work-force, depending on the study and the profession.

- The United States Census shows that the number of children being cared for by stay-at-home moms has increased nearly 13% in less than a decade, while at the same time, the percentage of new mothers who go back to work fell from 59% in 1998 to 55% in 2000.

- Working mothers between the career-building ages of 25 to 44—Two thirds of them work fewer than 40 hours per week (i.e., part time). Only 5% work 50 or more hours weekly.

- Compare these trends with those of men. 95% of white men with M.B.A.'s [master of business administration] are working full time, while only 67% of women with M.B.A.'s are working full time.

- Ms Belkin then turns her attention to the women in her Atlanta book club, and the roomful of women from Princeton University, "trained as well as any man. Of the 10 members, half are not working at all; one is in business with her husband; one works part time; two freelance; and the only one with a full-time job has no children."

- In a recent survey, the research firm Catalyst found that 26 percent of women at the cusp of the most senior levels of management don't want the promotion.

- *Fortune* magazine found that of the 108 women who have appeared on its list of the top 50 most powerful women over the years, at least 20 have chosen to leave their high-powered jobs, most voluntarily, for lives that are less intense and more fulfilling.

Perhaps the mechanism behind this trend can be explained in two words—"escape hatch." Ms Belkin quotes one of her interviewees: "I don't want to be famous; I don't want to conquer the world; I don't want that kind of life . . . Maternity provides an escape hatch that paternity does not. Having a baby provides a graceful and convenient exit."

Men Succumb to Social Pressures

Ms Belkin refers to women social scientists who write about "how the workplace has failed women." And then she observes that "it is also that women are rejecting the workplace."

Closing off her article with a twist to her original question about women running the world, Ms Belkin again asks why don't women run the world, and has one of her subjects answer it for her: "In a way," Amsbary says, "we really do."

Indeed. Women always have. Chivalrous, chauvinistic men (whose pro-feminism is a clever strategic move) believe that they wield the power—the so-called "frontman fallacy." But in so many ways, they are deluded. Is a draft-horse pulling the cart more powerful than the driver wielding the whip? Does a guard dog patrolling the yard determine how its owner should live? How much power does a draft horse or a guard dog have over its own destiny? When a man dutifully and willingly subscribes to the provider role, he becomes a beast of burden whose first priority is to conform to the rules laid down not only by his employer but also by his wife and the social network that is her priority.

Ms Belkin concludes her lengthy article with a positive spin, by suggesting that "instead of women being forced to act like men, men are being freed to act like women . . . Looked at that way, this is not the failure of a revolution, but the start of a new one. It is about a door opened but a crack by women that could usher in a new environment for us all."

Feminism Harms the Family

The fight for women's rights has actually turned into a fight against the family. Even the mothers of modern feminism admit that radical feminists have worked hard to repudiate the family. . . .

If we are going to fix our social problems, we must recognize that feminism has led our Western families into serious crises. Here is how it happened. Although many young women answered the call to pursue a career, they could not deny their natural desire for a husband and children. Many then opted to have a husband, children and a career. Realizing that certain feminine desires could not be denied, a new movement slogan was quickly pushed into public view—"having it all." This slogan lives on. But it ignores a hard reality for many working mothers: Having it all also means handling it all. Working career mothers were forced into a high-stress rat race. Having it all was supposed to be fulfilling, but it was not. Now, almost four decades later, women find they are not any closer to finding true, satisfying fulfillment. For some, "having it all" has meant losing it all.

The truth is, working mothers suffer. The children of working mothers always suffer. And should we forget— the husband suffers too.

Trumpet,
"How Feminism Harms Families,"
June/July 2006.

This is the basis of her message—a new revolution for which women can claim the credit, that benefits both men and women.

Insult to Men and Their Achievements

While we would not wish to diminish the important and worthwhile goal of motherhood that must feature in every woman's life decisions at some point, what Ms Belkin's article points to is a demonstration of the baselessness of the wage gap assumption. Hers is a most important admission that yes, many women—even once they have attained their status as equals among men (albeit, with the helping hand of affirmative action)—do not really want to work. Even with all the qualifications, skill bases and social connections that might make them heads of national corporations and leaders of nations, many women choose to throw it all in. Nothing wrong with that in principle, *except that every last woman in such a position has obtained her exulted status through affirmative action.* That is, through the assumption that, as a woman, she has the right to make her claim for the millennia of patriarchal oppression foisted against women by men. It's payback time. Payback for what?

Irrespective of what we make of Ms Belkin's positive spin, we are left with very troubling questions.

What do we make of this collective arrogance? For these career grrrls [alternative spelling of *girl*, popularized during the 1990s Riot Grrrl feminist punk movement] to decide that they've had enough, and then continue to disparage men and men's achievements by suggesting that they might have a more lofty purpose (motherhood). How insulting, to suggest that all this benefits men. These born-again moms are like occupying colonials trying to mollify the natives who have begun to show signs of becoming restless.

Whatever happened to the glass ceiling? Was it ever there to begin with? And now that progressive career grrrls have changed their minds, now that they realized that work was not all that it was cracked up to be, they white-wash it all with claims that everybody benefits, including men, because now men can be stay-at-home dads if they want to.

All this might be well and good for some. But let us not forget the propaganda with which this new, purported vision was accomplished. Let us not forget the hatred that has been leveled against men and "The Patriarchy" in order to realize these goals. Now that we realize that the wage gap is in fact a choices gap driven as much by women as by men—and Ms Belkin's article further confirms this already established fact—how do we justify the hatred and systemic biases that have been instituted against men over the past 40 years?

Propagating Hatred Against Men

These career women that Ms Belkin writes about (and among whom she includes herself) might as well have said, "hey, we never meant it." Or perhaps, "lighten up guys, we were just joking." Or maybe, "it's a woman's prerogative to change her mind."

How do we interpret the past 40 years of feminist hatred against an entire gender—men and boys, husbands and sons—how is this justified? Why have so many women remained silent accomplices? Whatever happened to respect? This fabricated claim, that a glass ceiling had been instituted in some secret conspiracy by "The Patriarchy" to deny women opportunities in the workplace, is the basis for affirmative action. But Ms Belkin's article further confirms that all this was a malicious lie—a lie that denied the efforts and contributions that have always been made by men and a lie against which so few women have spoken out. Even now, Ms Belkin does not speak out against the lie, but seeks only to justify the choices that she and others like her have made.

There never has been any such thing as a glass ceiling preventing women from getting ahead. There has always been chivalry, placing the burden upon men to be provider, cannon fodder and all-round chump-horse doing the bidding of women, entertaining women and fulfilling women's every whim.

Affirmative Action Against Men

In October 2001, following on the terrorist attack on the twin towers in New York, the US Department of Justice announced that it was dropping its support of a sex discrimination lawsuit by women sitting for a test for Philadelphia's transit police, who claimed that it was unfair to female applicants. It would appear that it took the event of September 11 to make everyone realize that there are some things (like carrying bodies up and down ladders) that women cannot do as well as men. In this light, Charlotte Allen suggests that it took the terrorist attack on New York to put an end to the worst excesses of affirmative action—meaning of course, affirmative action against men. . . .

The essence and status of affirmative action, at least prior to the September 11 attack, was typified in the *Washington Post* article by Dan Froomkin (October 1998), "Affirmative Action Under Attack":

> Affirmative action is the nation's most ambitious attempt to redress its long history of racial and sexual discrimination. But these days it seems to incite, rather than ease, the nation's internal divisions.
>
> An increasingly assertive opposition movement argues that the battle to guarantee equal rights for all citizens has been fought and won—and that favoring members of one group over another simply goes against the American grain.
>
> But defenders of affirmative action say that the playing field is not level yet—and that granting modest advantages to minorities and women is more than fair, given hundreds of years of discrimination that benefited whites and men.

Men, Not Women, Require Redress

Which brings us back to the wage gap myth and Ms Belkin's article. As we've explored above:

- The wage gap has been thoroughly debunked and certified non-existent.

- Ms Belkin's article above tells us how high-flying women with MBAs and law degrees flee their cherished careers because, well, it's just too hard, and women with more worthy priorities can do without the stress.

What does this all imply for the institutional bias against men, framed in the terms of Affirmative Action? If, as various sources confirm, wage differences have typically arisen from the choices that men and women made and not from discrimination, what is all this blather about women being discriminated against in the workplace by men? Redress for "hundreds of years of discrimination that benefited whites and men?" Indeed.

Yes, redress is indeed required. Men require redress for 40 years of feminist, hate-filled propaganda, vilification and harassment. Not all men, of course—for ultimately, chivalrous, powerful men continue to dominate the highest levels in the boardrooms, judiciary, industry and government, and they continue to do the bidding of feminists—as has always been the case even before modern feminism, when chivalrous men did the bidding of their women-folk. It is the men lower down in the hierarchies—unskilled men, skilled and educated men, men of integrity, men who for whatever reason refuse to play by the contemptible rules—that require redress for an unprecedented and unjustified campaign directed against them over the past 40 years.

It should become clear by now that affirmative action is just good, old-fashioned chivalry, pure and simple. Where before, we used to open car doors for the li'l ladies, presumably because they could not open car doors themselves, today we let them in front of us in the job queue, presumably because they cannot compete on their own merits. . . .

Affirmative Action Built on a Lie

Suffice it to say that affirmative action, as one tool within the feminist arsenal of anti-male hatred, is built on a lie. . . . Feminism is a hate movement. Its premise grounded primarily in the wage gap has been proven as baseless, and its agenda directed at maintaining privileges for women by way of affirmative action is a con. We must conclude that women have never been systematically discriminated against in any patriarchal conspiracy perpetrated by men. Rather, men have maintained the tradition of chivalry, to provide for women, and this has exempted women from *having* to work. This escape hatch that is every woman's birthright is what is responsible for the wage gap.

"The glass ceiling remains firmly in place."

The Glass Ceiling in Politics Needs to Be Shattered

Marie Cocco

The presidential election of 2008 saw former New York senator Hillary Clinton run as a candidate for the Democratic Party, while the Republican Party nominated Alaska governor Sarah Palin as its vice presidential candidate. Although heralded by many as a breakthrough year for women in politics, Marie Cocco argues that even though these women headed highly competitive and successful campaigns running for the highest government offices in the country, neither was elected, proving that the political glass ceiling remains firmly in place. Cocco also states that the number of women holding government positions—as governors, in Congress, and in the Cabinet—still lags far behind the number of men, highlighting the political inequality that she believes still exists in the United States. Marie Cocco is a Washington Post *journalist whose columns often focus on government policy and other current national issues.*

As you read, consider the following questions:

1. Why is the appointment of a woman to secretary of state insignificant in advancing women in politics, according to Cocco?

2. How many women does the author state will be governors in 2009?

3. What is the difference, identified by Barbara Lee and cited by Cocco, between the way that voters judge men and women?

It is time to stop kidding ourselves. This wasn't a breakthrough year for American women in politics. It was a brutal one.

The glass ceiling remains firmly in place—not cracked, as Hillary Clinton insisted as she tried to claim rhetorical victory after her defeat in the Democratic nominating contest. It wasn't even scratched with the candidacy of Sarah Palin as the Republican vice presidential nominee—unless you consider becoming an object of national ridicule to be a symbol of advancement. As divergent as these two women are ideologically and temperamentally, as different as are their résumés, they both banged their heads—hard—against the ceiling. Both were bruised. So was the goal of advancing women in political leadership.

Even if President-elect Barack Obama chooses Clinton as secretary of state, no ground will be broken. Clinton would be the third woman to hold the post. And there is no longer anything extraordinary in a president naming women to his Cabinet. Franklin D. Roosevelt did it first, when he appointed Frances Perkins as labor secretary in 1933. Since then, every president but Harry Truman and John F. Kennedy has named women to the Cabinet or to Cabinet-level posts, according to the Center for American Women and Politics at Rutgers Uni-

"Countries that have already had female heads of state" Hillary and Bill Clinton Cartoon. ©distributed by Universal Press Syndicate. Reproduced with permission of Universal Press Syndicate.

versity. Bill Clinton holds the record: He appointed 16 women overall, and at one point about half of those serving in Clinton's Cabinet were female.

But, we are invariably told, surely there are enough women moving through the "pipeline" of lower offices so that someday, some woman from *somewhere* will win the presidency or the vice presidency. Well, here is how things stand: Eight women will serve as governors in 2009, the same as this year. The proportion of women serving in statewide elective office actually has dropped since it reached a high of about 28 percent in 2000; it is now about 24 percent, according to the center.

The Senate will add one woman, bringing the number of female senators to 17. Ten newly elected House members are female. This means that as the class of 2008 enters the Capitol's marble halls, it will include less than half the number of women who first won office in 1992—the so-called "year of the woman."

Including incumbents and newcomers, a record number of women will be serving in Congress, but still only 17 percent of its members will be female. This is where that record places us: on a par with the legislative representation women have achieved in sub-Saharan Africa, Latin America and the Caribbean. The United Nations, which tracks women's global political advancement, says that at this rate, it will take women in the developing world 40 years to reach parity with men.

How long will it take us? We already are well into the fourth decade since the contemporary women's movement of the 1970s spawned a generation that sought to claim an equal place in the halls of power.

Those who watched the media's sexist hazing of both Clinton and Palin often rationalize this treatment as the result of these two candidates' particular personalities and the legitimacy—or presumed illegitimacy—of their campaigns. But Barbara Lee, whose Boston-based family foundation has conducted extensive research of gubernatorial races involving women, routinely identifies the same undercurrents in state campaigns. Voters demand more experience of a woman candidate, and judge her competence separately from whether she is sufficiently "likable." Male candidates typically must clear only the competence bar to be judged—as Obama indelicately put it during a primary debate—"likable enough."

"We heard that over and over again—that no woman is ever right," Lee says of her focus groups. "They like the concept of it but when it comes to a real, live, breathing candidate, they don't."

Lee summarizes the disparate assessment this way: "There are no female Arnold Schwarzeneggers." That is, no woman will ever burst into politics, capture the voters' imagination and be catapulted into high public office without a lick of experience.

Yet American women are a majority of the population and a majority of the electorate. They earn more than half the bachelor's and master's degrees, a level of educational achievement far exceeding that of women in developing countries. There must be some reason we don't do any better than women in impoverished, rural regions of the world where cultural norms oppress women.

Maybe it is because our culture isn't so different after all.

| "There are no [political] positions that women cannot fill."

The Glass Ceiling in Politics Has Been Shattered

Michelle D. Bernard

In August 2008, then-governor of Alaska Sarah Palin was chosen to be the vice presidential candidate of the Republican Party to run alongside Arizona senator John McCain. Michelle D. Bernard, president and chief executive officer of the Independent Women's Forum and Independent Women's Voice, argues in the following viewpoint that Palin's candidacy attests to the fact that women have shattered the political glass ceiling and that a woman will soon be president of the United States. Bernard believes that the increasing participation of women in politics and the diversifying views of successful female politicians—from feminist liberals to free market conservatives—further support the notion that women are empowered individuals investing all parts of the political process. Bernard's Independent Women's Forum is a public policy organization promoting traditionally conservative ideals such as limited government, free markets, and strong families.

Michelle D. Bernard, "The Sarah Palin Effect: Shattering America's Political Glass Ceiling," *Independent Women's Forum*, November 10, 2008. Reproduced with permission by Independent Women's Forum. www.iwf.org.

As you read, consider the following questions:

1. Who are some of the successful women politicians mentioned by Bernard, and what positions have they held?

2. Who does Bernard accuse of being the most vicious critics of Sarah Palin?

3. What stereotype does the author believe Palin broke during the 2008 presidential campaign?

America's political glass ceiling was shattered yesterday [November 4, 2008]. True, Sarah Palin wasn't elected vice president, but her presence on the Republican ticket in this historic campaign is further evidence that the final barrier will soon be overcome, whether by her, Sen. Hillary Clinton [who competed in the 2008 Democratic presidential primary], or someone else.

There are no other political limits facing women. Nancy Pelosi [Democratic congresswoman from California] serves as Speaker of the US House of Representatives. Condoleezza Rice served (as did Madeleine Albright before her) as the US Secretary of State [under George W. Bush]. Women routinely serve as Senators, governors (like Sarah Palin), and cabinet officers. There are no positions that women cannot fill.

Those eager for a woman in the White House should also find comfort in Senator [Barack] Obama's victory. He has demonstrated that all Americans, regardless of the discrimination suffered by their ancestors, now can grasp our nation's bountiful opportunities as their own.

Tenacity Facing Unrelenting Attacks

This wasn't an easy campaign. Even before she joined Senator [John] McCain in this presidential campaign, Governor Palin had demonstrated that she was an accomplished politician: she defeated the incumbent governor in her state's primary and a former governor in the general election. Her knowledge of international affairs might be limited, but she beat Alaska's political establishment, learned the intricacies of the state's dominant energy industry, and put her stamp on state government—all the while caring for a husband and five children.

Her evident tenacity served her well. Before the election, she acknowledged to *Good Morning America*'s Elizabeth Vargas that "the constant barrage, a kind of spin on my record or my positions" could "change someone's perceptions" and was the likely reason her support among women fell about 40 percent.

There were bountiful substantive issues dividing the candidates, all of which warranted a thorough and even tough debate. But some of the attacks on Governor Palin were blatantly sexist cheap shots—questions about how she could be both mother and vice president, for instance. Some of her angriest critics were vicious and vulgar, substituting profanity for argument. Many of these attacks came from many so-called feminists.

This isn't the first time that American democracy fell short of the ideal. Nevertheless, the level of vitriol was disheartening. Frankly, all Americans should be celebrating the unprecedented diversity exhibited in the 2008 election. A white woman [Clinton] and black man [Obama] battling for the nomination of one party; a war hero and oldest presidential candidate [McCain] ever winning the other party's contest. A woman [Palin] chosen as one of the vice presidential nominees.

Women Politicians Not All Liberal

Thankfully, Palin refused to fold under pressure, explaining to Vargas that she would not "give up and wave a white flag of surrender against some of the political shots that we've taken." Even though her team didn't win, Sarah Palin is a symbol of women's progress. America's daughters, as well as sons, now truly can aspire to hold the highest office in the land.

Women Control Congress

Nancy Pelosi, who has served as San Francisco's Democratic congresswoman since 1987, is . . . the most powerful woman in elective office in American history. As Speaker of the House, the 66-year-old mother of five and grandmother of six will be third in line to the presidency. But despite the obvious newsworthiness of Pelosi's ascent, it may not be the most significant gain made by women. . . .

More noteworthy is that the female newcomers [to Congress] belong almost exclusively to the incoming Democratic majority—both new senators and eight of the 10 congresswomen. In the Senate, the women make up just under a quarter of the Democratic caucus, and comprise 21 percent of the Democrats in the House.

But what truly marks the 2006 midterms as a watershed for women in politics is the astounding degree to which women in both the House and Senate are now moving up into positions of power, in the leadership and at the head of key committees and subcommittees. Democratic women appear finally to have broken through what Pelosi calls the "marble ceiling." Women will not just be represented in the new Congress—to a remarkable extent, they will be running the place.

Clara Bingham, Washington Monthly, *January/February 2007.*

In the process, Gov. Palin has dramatically busted another stereotype: the presumption that a feminist and career-oriented woman must be a political liberal. Indeed, much of the venom spewed at candidate Palin reflected liberal frustration that this woman running for vice president was—gasp!—a conservative, free market feminist.

Senator Clinton is an intelligent and accomplished woman, but she came to prominence and won her first election to the Senate based on her husband's coattails. Her service in the Senate has left no doubt about her qualifications to sit in the Oval Office, but she had advantages before her first political race that Governor Palin could only dream of.

However, Senator Clinton's more important credential—at least from the standpoint of big government feminists and left-wing political activists—was that she was a liberal. Almost by definition that was seen as qualifying her to hold high political office. Feminism and liberalism were considered to be two sides of a single coin.

Governor Palin has wrecked this convenient assumption on the left. Women, no less than men, vary in their political opinions. Many women view both family and career as important. Many women believe in a free society which protects individual liberty, limits government, and rewards enterprise. Many women consider abortion to be an affront to the sacredness of innocent life which society—including women—is called upon to defend. It's fine to disagree with some or all of these opinions. But there is no "right" position for women.

A Woman President Soon

We should all wish Sarah Palin well. Whether or not we voted for her, we all benefit from her presence in this hard fought campaign.

American women, whether liberal or conservative, should be proud. No one knows what her political future will be—if she will one day run herself for the White House—but there is something we do know: having a woman in the White House is only a matter of time.

Periodical Bibliography

The following articles have been selected to supplement the diverse views presented in this chapter.

Nancy C. Andrews
"Climbing Through Medicine's Glass Ceiling," *New England Journal of Medicine*, November 8, 2007.

Michael Applebaum
"Beyond the Glass Ceiling," *Brandweek*, September 11, 2006.

Katie Baker
"Cracking the Highest Glass Ceiling," *Newsweek*, October 6, 2008.

Robert Drago
"Harvard and the Academic Glass Ceiling," *Chronicle of Higher Education*, March 30, 2007.

Sean Gregory
"Uneven Playing Field," *Time*, August 27, 2007.

Susan Hansen
"Cracks in the Glass Ceiling?" *Sex Roles*, May 2009.

Bill Pennington
"Colleges: Study May Fuel Debate over Title IX's Effect on Men's Sports," *New York Times*, June 6, 2007.

René Street and Carolyn Elman
"Shattering the Glass Ceiling," *Women in Business*, April/May 2009.

Mark Trumbull
"For Women, Glass Ceiling Still an Issue," *Christian Science Monitor*, February 8, 2007.

Susannah Tully
"What Barriers Hold Women Back?" *Chronicle of Higher Education*, December 21, 2007.

Mark Walsh
"Sex-Bias Remedies Upheld," *Education Week*, January 28, 2009.

CHAPTER 4

What Global Policies Promote Social Justice?

Chapter Preface

In late 1999, then-secretary general of the United Nations Kofi Annan declared that as the world prepared to leave the twentieth century behind, it would have to decide whether the ravages of warfare exemplified in the first half of the century would be repeated in the next century or whether the peace and expansion of trade that marked the second half of the twentieth century would dominate the new era. He hoped the developed countries would see the advantages of aiding developing nations in building their economies through free and fair trade, so that the disparity between rich and poor states could be reduced and all the world could benefit from increased prosperity.

Increasing trade and development, however, may not be the cure-all for bringing economic justice to the so-called third world. The World Bank has often noted in its annual World Development Report that even if developing nations maintained a high gross domestic product growth rate of 2 percent per year, their per capita incomes would still lag far behind those of the world's economic leaders for the foreseeable future. World Bank economists contend that while globalization may be helping open new trade routes into developing nations, it is the capability to innovate that will spur growth in the third world. Vikram Nehru, a chief economist in Asian markets, explains that innovation in this context refers to "not only the capability of creating new technologies, but also of disseminating, adapting and adopting existing technologies." Although economists are aware that many developing nations lack appropriate infrastructure to innovate in all areas, they do believe that some technological innovations can provide steps up for these countries. And global corporations are willing to feed these new markets.

"Nokia, for one, has for several years seen most of its growth come from the developing world, so it was quick to notice when poor Kenyans started using their cell phones for banking as well as paying for things," reports Michael Fitzgerald for the business Web site Fast Company. What Nokia recognized was that Kenyans—who did not own many computers on which to do their banking—were quick to pick up and embrace the new cell phone banking technology. Writing for the *Boston Globe*, Jeremy Kahn notes that second and third world markets are often treated to cutting edge design before first world nations even hear of it. He reports that a new smart card technology is being unveiled in India that allows citizens to bank by mobile phone. Kahn states that the smart card technology "is so advanced that it isn't available to even the most tech-savvy Americans—at least not yet." Kahn and others say that many high-tech global firms are using developing countries as testing grounds for products, giving those regions a first look at the latest communication systems, banking technology, and consumer products. Kahn even claims that many third world governments are investing in the latest technologies because they have no reliance on older, outdated systems. First world nations, on the other hand, must pay for the costs of innovation often by removing old networks and machines, and sometimes the benefits are not worth the price. As Kahn writes, "In many cases, it is mature markets like the United States and Europe, tethered to older systems, that find themselves playing catch-up."

Whether innovation will speed social justice in global economies is still a matter of debate. Many other factors hamper the progress of development for struggling markets. In the following chapter, experts examine some of the issues that developing nations face on the path toward social and economic improvement.

"What has caused greater economic integration between nations—and this is often forgotten or deliberately overlooked by the critics of globalisation—is individuals taking decision in pursuit of their own interests and being given the liberty to [do] so."

Globalization Is Increasing Social Justice

Alexander Downer

Alexander Downer served as Australia's foreign minister for eleven years, stepping down in 2007. He makes clear his feelings about globalization in the following viewpoint, a commencement address given to Bond University graduates. Downer claims that globalization has lifted many people in developing nations out of poverty and provided them with access to health care and education, which is an increase in social justice. In developed nations, globalization has lowered unemployment and raised incomes, Downer asserts. Overall, Downer insists that globalization gives people economic freedom to further their own interests—whether to start businesses or to take advantage of the diverse products the world has to offer.

Alexander Downer, "Globalisation: A Force for Good," speech delivered at Bond University, Australia, February 4, 2006. Reproduced by permission.

As you read, consider the following questions:

1. How does Downer define globalization?

2. In East Asia, what does the author say happens to the income of the poor when the economy grows by 1 percent?

3. How has retreating from globalization affected Zimbabwe, according to Downer?

What do we mean by globalisation?

The World Bank describes it as "the growing integration of economies and societies around the world." Essentially, people and countries are more interconnected. What happens in one country can influence another. Wall Street sneezes and the rest of the world catches a cold.

Technology advancements, in the form of rapidly reduced transportation and communication costs, combined with policy decisions to reduce trade and investment barriers have been important factors behind this rapid global integration in recent decades. But they have not *caused* globalisation to occur.

What has *caused* greater economic integration between nations—and this is often forgotten or deliberately overlooked by the critics of globalisation—is individuals taking decision in pursuit of their own interests and being given the liberty to [do] so. A McDonalds restaurant for example—enemy number one to the anti-globalisation forces—only exists because there are people who freely choose to open the restaurant and because there are people who freely choose to purchase meals at the restaurant.

Australia imports clothing from Bangladesh because there are Bangladeshis who freely choose to sell their products abroad and because there are Australians who freely choose to purchase them. Lower transportation costs and lower tariffs on imported goods into Australia allow this to occur more easily, but no trade would occur without the free choice of individuals on both sides. Likewise, Australia's exports of wine to Britain don't occur because of any government mandate, but, again, because of the free choices of thousands of people both producing the wine and consuming it and being given the freedom by governments to do so.

Opening a McDonalds, importing clothes from Bangladesh, exporting wine to Britain. All of these things result in greater global economic integration, or globalisation. And they are all caused by people being given the freedom to pursue their own interests. This alone is a very powerful argument in support of globalisation.

What Historical Evidence Shows

To limit the freedom of individuals to pursue their own interests requires very convincing evidence that such freedom has very negative consequences on the broader society. Many critics will claim exactly this, citing poorer people as having particularly suffered. An impassionate view of the evidence, however, suggests otherwise.

Consider what has occurred over the last century and particularly the last 20 to 40 years, which coincides with the acceleration of greater global integration. The past century has seen more people lifted out of poverty than in all of human history. In 1820, about 85% of the world's population were living in absolute poverty—usually defined as living on less than one dollar a day. By 1950 that figure had fallen to 50%. Today it is about 20%. Swedish economist, Johan Norberg, notes that in the last 20 years, for the first time in history, both the proportion and the absolute number of people living in absolute poverty has declined. The population grew by 1.5 billion while the number living in absolute poverty fell by 200 million.

Cutting Poverty in Half

There is substantial evidence, from countries of different sizes and different regions, that as countries "globalize" their citizens benefit, in the form of access to a wider variety of goods and services, lower prices, more and better-paying jobs, improved health, and higher overall living standards. It is probably no mere coincidence that over the past 20 years, as a number of countries have become more open to global economic forces, the percentage of the developing world living in extreme poverty—defined as living on less than $1 per day—has been cut in half.

International Monetary Fund Issues Brief, May 2008.

The average global income per capita has almost doubled over the last 35 years with the poorest fifth of the population increasing their income faster than the wealthiest fifth. Life expectancies show a similar pattern. At the start of the 20th century, life expectancy in developing countries was 35 years. By the end of the century it was 65. . . . Infant mortality rates are half what they were in 1970. Adult illiteracy has almost halved.

This is phenomenal, unprecedented progress and it did not happen by accident or in spite of globalisation. Rather it occurred as a result of increased economic growth due to the opening up of economies and the spreading of global capitalism.

Capitalism Brings Many Benefits

Studies have shown that the more open economies and those that have most successfully integrated with the global economy have produced the best growth results, while those that have remained closed have produced the worst. For example, a

2002 World Bank study of 72 developing countries found that since 1980, the "globalisers"—those that increased their ratio of trade to GDP [gross domestic product]—grew almost four times faster than non-globalisers. A further study estimated that an increase in the ratio of trade to GDP by one percent raises the level of income by one-half to two percent.

East Asian Gains

Our regional neighbours have been some of the big gainers from globalisation. From the 1960s onwards, most East Asian economies became increasingly export oriented and globalised, lowering tariffs and expanding their trade. They also provided their populations education and infrastructure and generally sound governance. As a result, per capita income grew most strongly in East Asian economies over the last 20 years.

In the 1990s, with the exception of Japan, East Asia grew by between 6–8 per cent per annum, and the share of regional populations living in poverty fell rapidly. Furthermore, the growth in these countries didn't just benefit a small few with the poor lagging behind as some people suggest. Rather, evidence shows that economic growth is on average associated one-for-one with higher incomes of the poor. That is, when an economy grows 1%, the incomes of the poor rise on average by one percent. There are exceptions to this, but statistical evidence shows that, on average, the poor have benefited at roughly the same speed as the rich.

Some Countries Are Left out

In contrast to the rapidly growing East Asian countries, countries that have failed to grow and still suffer desperate poverty—most notably many countries in sub-Saharan Africa—have failed to integrate into the world economy. This failure to integrate is caused by domestic conditions including war and internal governance, but it is sometimes made worse by rich countries putting up barriers to their products, particularly farm products. As UN Secretary General Kofi Annan has said: "The main losers in today's very unequal world are not those that are too much exposed to globalisation. They are those that have been left out."

Zimbabwe and Australia

For those who are still in doubt, it is worth reflecting on what happens when a country closes its doors having been opened to the world for some time. Zimbabwe is probably the best illustration of this.

According to Norberg, Zimbabwe has "undertaken the world's fastest and most consistent retreat from the alleged evils of globalisation and liberalisation." Under [Zimbabwe's president] Robert Mugabe, trade has been limited, government spending has increased, price controls installed, freedom of expression limited, and property appropriated. The result? Within 5 years, Zimbabwe went from being an exporter of foodstuffs to a country where more than 6 million people were facing starvation.

Australia, of course, has been both at the fore-front of, and a beneficiary of globalisation. Over the last 20 years, the Australian Government has cut tariffs, opened itself up to global capital markets and implemented significant micro-economic reform. While this has resulted in some significant disruption to some industries, Australia overall has benefited profoundly with productivity growth in the second half of the 1990s 40 percent higher than in the 1970s and 80s. This has led to higher incomes and the lowest unemployment levels in decades.

Keeping the Gains

It is worth remembering that lowering trade and investment barriers is necessary, but not sufficient, to ensure that communities keep and spread the gains from globalisation. Governments must also ensure domestic goods, labour and financial markets work and legal systems and infrastructure function efficiently. They must operate stable macroeconomic policies to keep inflation low and employment full. And they must ensure that their populations have access to good quality education and health care and adequate social safety nets.

| "Globalisation has done no good to the poor."

Globalization Is Not Increasing Social Justice

Binoy Barman

In the following viewpoint, Professor Binoy Barman, head of the English department at Daffodil International University in Bangladesh, explains what he believes are the negative effects of globalization. Barman sees globalization as a tool of the dominant West and its corporations, forcing capitalism and its consumer values on the rest of the world. In Barman's opinion, globalization is threatening to destroy indigenous cultures and brings misery to the workers and the poor who are trapped at the bottom of the economic ladder.

As you read, consider the following questions:

1. In Barman's opinion, how has globalization made the human soul sick?

2. According to the author, how has globalization impacted terrorism?

3. How has globalization affected farmers, according to Barman?

Globalisation has gobbled the whole world. There is virtually no part on earth which has not been hit and bit by the enormous fangs of the monster. All aspects of life have come under the sinister impact of globalisation, growing and dwelling in the shadow of capitalism. It dazzles like the sun and blinds normal vision. With its apparent grandeur, it ensnares people, though it is hollow in its core. I doubt globalisation will lead us to a better future, bringing well-being for the common folks.

I was thinking of the globalised perils while listening to [Bangladeshi] Professor Dr. Fakrul Alam on "Postcolonialism in the age of globalisation" at AIUB [the American International University-Bangladesh] on March 17 [2009]. In fact, the word "globalisation," a buzzword nowadays, attracted me to what the organisers called [an] "interactive colloquium."

Professor Alam talked eloquently on postcolonial literature and its background and development, clearly delineating its connection with present-day world order. Literature has assumed new dimension in recent decades in the face of globalisation, focussing on issues like diaspora, hybridity and cosmopolitan culture.

An Empty Promise

He said that globalisation was ushering in a system of "internationalism," dismantling the barriers of narrow nationalism. So the dream of a "world without borders" hovers over the horizon. It holds a promise for many, like the revered Professor Alam. But to me, the promise is empty.

Globalisation has brought more hazards than comforts. A mechanical and materialistic view of life has been imported and incorporated, through the vehicle of globalisation, into oriental space hitherto basking in the complacency of idealism. It has gnawed at the ethical base of this region. It has been a great loss for humanity, I should say, a colossal moral defeat.

Globalisation preaches the philosophy of hedonism. Consumer goods are spread around and a mantra is whispered; "Consume, consume and consume. You have no work other than consumption!" Thus, globalisation has made the human soul spiritually sick, morally bankrupt and intellectually pretentious.

Globalisation has posed a genuine threat to indigenous culture and language across the globe. The dominant culture is out there to suppress the meek and mild. The affected, with the loss of their culture and language, fall into a vacuum, suffering from an identity crisis.

They become alienated from and in themselves. Some may take it as a harmless outcome of the spontaneous interaction between multifarious cultural and linguistic elements while others may see it as the consequence of cultural and linguistic imperialism or aggression.

Globalisation has taught the world corporate trickery. The West is the breeding ground of big corporate scandals. Corporate culture seeks to influence the government machinery through fraudulence and corruption for the interest of the vested quarters, the bourgeoisie. It promotes the motto of maximising profit, by fair means or foul. It suggests a heartless handling of business affairs, where human life carries no value.

Life becomes a mere commodity. Money stands at the centre of all activities. Everybody runs after money when money itself is not stationary. It flows to the people who have already got enough. It is not meant for the penniless. Globalisation is for the gentlemen; there is no hope for the subaltern, the marginalised.

Globalisation has globalised terrorism, in a literal sense. The root of terrorism does not lie in the soil of the East but

The Threat of McWorld

Neoliberal globalisation is not just a matter of economics; it also threatens entire ways of life. The global penetration of the mass media and the values, images and tastes they purvey, have a powerful impact upon non-Western cultures. Television, films, popular music and advertising, industries dominated by US mega-corporations, pervade the world. These industries transmit a possessive individualism that fragments tightly knit communities; propagate consumer tastes that influence the dress, language, food and attitudes of young people; popularise notions of sexual, gender and authority relations that often clash with local notions of virtuous behaviour; and reflect a secular, narcissistic outlook usually in conflict with sacred worldviews defended by local elites. . . .

The dialectical reaction to 'McWorld'—the homogenising, consumer-orientated and secular popular culture—is often 'Jihad'—a reversion to a world defined by religion, hierarchy and tradition.

Richard Sandbrook and David Romano,
Third World Quarterly, *vol. 25, no. 6, 2004.*

of the West. The capitalist West used the gullible oriental people to implement its heinous political design. It gave arms to fundamentalists and set them to combat the forces of the proletariat.

Unfortunately, the gun is now directed back to the provocative West, hence the fundamentalists have been given the epithet "terrorists." It is the West that is completely responsible for the development and spread of what we call "terrorism."

The Rich Get Richer

Globalisation has done no good to the poor. It has made farmers dependent on genetically modified seeds produced by the technologically advanced nations. It has dragged workers from one geographical location to another, often dumping them in more repressive working environments. The labourers only change zones, without much uplift in status.

This "dislocated labour" serves the rich, the manufacturers, the giant corporations. In the process, slave remains slave and master remains master. Globalisation turns daily necessities dearer, almost out of the reach of the poor. And, if anybody has to die from hunger in the days of soaring prices, it is the poor peasants and workers, the downtrodden, first.

At the state level, globalisation only feeds the economy of rich nations. The industrialised countries sell their "unsellable" products to the hungry population of the underdeveloped or developing countries and earn undue profit. The balance of trade is tilted, without any exception, towards the heavyweights.

The so-called least developed countries have no chance to score high in the free field of free market. The ball is always in the court of skilled players. Even the legislations of WTO [the World Trade Organization] cannot guarantee the interest of poor citizens of the world. Alas! [eighteenth-century economist] Adam Smith, what damage have you caused to humanity with your *Wealth of Nations*, paving the way for laissez-faire!

As the craze of globalisation rages on, our problems are only globalised, while there are no globalised solutions. We may go round and round the globe, like a merry-go-round, reaching nowhere. Simply there is no way. No emancipation from globalisation. With this new realisation, I think, literature should play a more critical role, shunning all enthusiasm for it, in identifying and overcoming the problems of globalisation. That is the sole duty of literary philosophy in the age of globalisation.

*"Those who contend that foreign aid
does not work—and cannot work—are
mistaken."*

Foreign Aid Benefits
Developing Nations

*Part I: Jeffrey Sachs; Part II: Raymond C. Offenheiser and
Rodney Bent*

*In part I of the following viewpoint, economist Jeffrey Sachs, the
director of the Earth Policy Institute at Columbia University and
the author of* The End of Poverty, *argues that U.S. foreign aid
is already helping impoverished African nations to improve agriculture, health care, and trade. He contends that the successes
should be built upon, and that more aid should be disbursed at,
the community level so that it can be measured and proven effective. In part II of the viewpoint, Raymond C. Offenheiser and
Rodney Bent further Sach's claims by stressing that foreign aid
must continue even during difficult financial times. Offenheiser
and Bent assert that the best way to help countries receiving aid
is to involve them in decision-making processes, allowing the recipients to determine how best to use the aid given. In the*

Part I: Jeffrey Sachs, "Foreign Aid Is in Everyone's Interest," *Christian Science Monitor*,
May 10, 2006, p. 9. Copyright © 2006 the Los Angeles Times. Reproduced by permission
of the author. Part II: Raymond C. Offenheiser and Rodney Bent "How to Make U.S.
Foreign Aid Work," *Christian Science Monitor*, vol. 101, March 18, 2009, p. 9. Copyright
© 2009 The Christian Science Monitor. Reproduced by permission of the authors.

authors' opinion, this will boost self-reliance and reinforce the notion that aid is a shared responsibility and not a hand out. Raymond C. Offenheiser is the president of Oxfam, an international relief organization. Rodney Bent is the acting chief executive officer of the Millennium Challenge Corporation, a U.S. government organization that aids countries in achieving sustained economic growth and responsible governance.

As you read, consider the following questions:

1. According to Sachs, what was the first step in Asia's ascent out of poverty?

2. What are the standards for successful aid, as Sachs defines them?

3. As Offenheiser and Bent explain, what is "country ownership" and why is it the best form of aid management?

The developing world often seems like highway traffic. Countries such as China, India, and Chile are in a slipstream of rapid economic growth, closing the technological gap with the industrialized countries, while nations such as Nepal, Niger, and Sudan are rushing in the reverse direction, with rising unrest, confrontation, drought, and disease.

The costs of the economic failures are enormous for the whole world because conflicts, terrorism, the drug trade, and refugees spill across national borders.

But drivers can change direction, and so can countries. India, China, and Chile were hardly success stories in the 1960s and 1970s. All were in turmoil, beset by poverty, hunger, and political instability. Their economic transformations show that today's "basket cases" can be tomorrow's emerging markets.

Escaping Poverty

Those who contend that foreign aid does not work—and cannot work—are mistaken. These skeptics make a career of promoting pessimism by pointing to the many undoubted failures of past aid efforts. But the fact remains that we can help ensure the successful economic development of the poorest countries. We can help them escape from poverty. It's in our national interest to do so.

The first step out of rural poverty almost always involves a boost in food production to end cycles of famine. Asia's ascent from poverty in the last 40 years began with a "green revolution." Food yields doubled or tripled. The Rockefeller Foundation helped with the development and propagation of high-yield seeds, and US aid enabled India and other countries to provide subsidized fertilizer and seeds to impoverished farmers. Once farmers could earn an income, they could move on to small-business development.

A second step out of poverty is an improvement in health conditions, led by improved nutrition, cleaner drinking water, and more basic health services. In the Asian success stories, child mortality dropped sharply, which, in turn, led to smaller families because poor parents gained confidence that their children would survive to adulthood.

The third step is the move from economic isolation to international trade. Chile, for instance, has become the chief source of off-season fruit in the US during the past 20 years by creating highly efficient supply chains. China and India have boomed as exporters of manufacturing goods and services, respectively. In all three, trade linkages were a matter of improved connectivity—roads, power, telecommunications, the Internet, and transport containerization.

Aid Working in Africa

Today, the skeptics like to claim that Africa is too far behind, too corrupt, to become a China or India. They are mistaken. An African green revolution, health revolution, and connectivity revolution are all within reach. Engineers and scientists have already developed the needed tools. The Millennium Villages project, which I and a group of colleagues developed, is

Millennium Challenge Corporation

Our partner countries are buzzing with the implementation activity of putting their MCC [Millennium Challenge Corporation] grants to work—activity that is multiplying every day. Projects implemented by our MCC partner countries have already resulted in more than 48,000 farmers being trained and more than 3,000 hectares of land under production so far. More than 3,000 kilometers of roads are under design. More than 600 kilometers of irrigation canals are being built. To date, MCC has committed over $6.7 billion to 35 countries worldwide to fund country-sourced programs to fight poverty through growth. Over $6.3 billion of this total has been awarded to 18 countries in Africa, Central America, Eurasia, and the Pacific that have passed our "good government" eligibility criteria to qualify for our sizable, five-year grants we call compacts. The remainder—in smaller grants—has been awarded through MCC's threshold program to countries that come close to passing and are firmly committed to improving their performance on our eligibility criteria.

John Danilovich,
remarks at Conrad N. Hilton Foundation Symposium,
October 20, 2008.

now rapidly expanding in 10 countries in Africa and is showing that this triple transformation—in improved agriculture, health, and connectivity—is feasible.

Improved seed varieties, fertilizers, irrigation, and trucks have all helped convert famine into bumper crops in just one or two productive growing seasons.

Malaria is under control. Farmers have access to capital to make the change from subsistence to cash crops. Children are being treated for worms and receive a midday meal to help keep them healthy and in school.

Skeptics said that African peasants would not grow more food, that fertilizers would go missing, that bed nets would be cut up to make wedding veils, and that local officials would block progress.

The truth is the opposite. In any part of the world, the poorest of the poor want a chance for a better future, especially for their children. Give them the tools, and they will grasp the chance.

Targeting Aid to Communities

Aid skeptics such as professor William Easterly, author of the recent book *The White Man's Burden*, are legion. Instead of pointing to failures, we need to amplify the successes—including the green revolution, the global eradication of small-pox, the spread of literacy, and, now, the promise of the Millennium Villages.

The standards for successful aid are clear. They should be targeted, specific, measurable, accountable, and scalable. They should support the triple transformation in agriculture, health, and infrastructure. We should provide direct assistance to villages in ways that can be measured and monitored.

The Millennium Village project relies on community participation and accountability to ensure that fertilizers, medicines, and the like are properly used.

Millennium Promise, an organization I cofounded, champions and furthers the development of the Millennium Villages project. It has partnered with the Red Cross, UNICEF [United Nations Children's Fund], the UN Foundation, Centers for Disease Control [and Prevention], and the World Health Organization to get antimalaria bed nets to the children of Africa.

In this fragile and conflict-laden world, we must value life everywhere by stopping needless disease and deaths, promoting economic growth, and helping ensure that our children's lives will be treasured in the years ahead.

President [Barack] Obama is ushering in a "new era of responsibility." And at this time of economic downturn it's a good thing. Every facet of the government's business, including how US tax dollars are invested in the fight against global poverty, must be treated with a renewed sense of responsibility.

The call to responsibility is a staple of American values, so why shouldn't it underscore the delivery of US development assistance? A clear majority of opinion leaders polled in a recent survey believe that foreign assistance and supporting development in poor countries should be used as a more important tool for US foreign policy in the Obama administration. As we pick up that duty, US taxpayer dollars have to be spent with a clear sense of purpose and accountability.

Involving Aid Recipients

One way to do that is to make sure that in this conversation we include an important ally in the fight for accountability— the recipients of US foreign assistance. Just as American taxpayers are concerned about how their money is spent, recipients of help in the form of money abroad want to know that they are getting the most value from each dollar spent. They can help us spend wisely.

Consider Honduras, which received a $215 million grant from the US government through the Millennium Challenge Corporation to fight poverty and stimulate economic growth.

Honduras is using the bulk of this funding to build roads to give farmers better access to markets and to let poor families reach schools and health clinics. To sustain this vital investment for the long-term benefit of its citizens, the country added its own funds for road maintenance.

It makes most sense to invest US development dollars in a way that lets recipients themselves champion home-grown solutions to their needs and hold their governments accountable for the results.

The international development community calls such country responsibility "country ownership," a concept experts agree makes development aid more effective. This sometimes means that the best way to get more accountability for taxpayers is to shift control to the people on the ground, where development actually happens, and away from Washington.

Self-Reliance and Responsibility

This fundamental realization is already changing how development aid is delivered and providing powerful lessons for defining its future. Country-led development makes sense as an American approach to assistance—one predicated on responsibility, self-reliance, entrepreneurship, and a firm belief in investments as a hand up, not a hand out.

Washington is taking due note and discussing ways toward a coherent development assistance strategy that recognizes the significance of country ownership in bringing about sustainable change in the lives of the world's poor.

America should stand firmly behind a common sense approach to aid effectiveness that incorporates country ownership, because poor countries know their development challenges best and local solutions are superior to the ones devised thousands of miles away.

Greater Global Prosperity

Striking a balance between helping poor people in developing countries and making US aid effective demands one thing: accountability. For aid to work well, power and responsibility need to rest not only with those providing it but also receiving it. What more American way is there to carry out our global responsibilities?

At a time when every dollar counts, the moment has come to heed the call to shared responsibility and instill the core value of country ownership in how US development assistance is delivered.

This is smart for America, smart for our partners, and smart for our drive toward greater opportunity and prosperity around the world.

| "Evidence overwhelmingly demonstrates
that aid to Africa has made the poor
poorer, and the growth slower."

Foreign Aid Harms
Developing Nations

Dambisa Moyo

*A native of Zambia, Dambisa Moyo holds a doctorate in eco-
nomics and a master's degree in finance. She has worked for bro-
kers and the World Bank, and she is the author of* Dead Aid:
Why Aid Is Not Working and How There Is a Better Way for
Africa. *In the following viewpoint, Moyo explains how foreign
aid has harmed, not helped Africa. In her view, aid has increased poor countries' debts, compelling these nations to focus
finances on debt repayment instead of on education, business
growth, and health care. Furthermore, she believes aid money is
fostering corruption in the governments of poor countries, leaving little assistance for the common people. Finally, Moyo contends that nonmonetary aid—such as surplus goods and foodstuffs—often flood indigenous markets, killing off local businesses
and making countries dependent on these handouts.*

As you read, consider the following questions:

1. According to Moyo, what percent of Africa's population lives on less than one dollar per day?

2. In the author's view, how does foreign aid keep bad African governments in power?

3. What suggestions does Moyo offer to help Africa?

A month ago I visited Kibera, the largest slum in Africa. This suburb of Nairobi, the capital of Kenya, is home to more than one million people, who eke out a living in an area of about one square mile—roughly 75% the size of New York's Central Park. It is a sea of aluminum and cardboard shacks that forgotten families call home. The idea of a slum conjures up an image of children playing amidst piles of garbage, with no running water and the rank, rife stench of sewage. Kibera does not disappoint.

What is incredibly disappointing is the fact that just a few yards from Kibera stands the headquarters of the United Nations' agency for human settlements which, with an annual budget of millions of dollars, is mandated to "promote socially and environmentally sustainable towns and cities with the goal of providing adequate shelter for all." Kibera festers in Kenya, a country that has one of the highest ratios of development workers per capita. This is also the country where in 2004, British envoy Sir Edward Clay apologized for underestimating the scale of government corruption and failing to speak out earlier.

Giving alms to Africa remains one of the biggest ideas of our time—millions march for it, governments are judged by it, celebrities proselytize the need for it. Calls for more aid to Africa are growing louder, with advocates pushing for doubling the roughly $50 billion of international assistance that already goes to Africa each year.

Yet evidence overwhelmingly demonstrates that aid to Africa has made the poor poorer, and the growth slower. The insidious aid culture has left African countries more debt-laden, more inflation-prone, more vulnerable to the vagaries of the currency markets and more unattractive to higher-quality investment. It's increased the risk of civil conflict and unrest (the fact that over 60% of sub-Saharan Africa's population is under the age of 24 with few economic prospects is a cause for worry). Aid is an unmitigated political, economic and humanitarian disaster.

Few will deny that there is a clear moral imperative for humanitarian and charity-based aid to step in when necessary, such as during the 2004 tsunami in Asia. Nevertheless, it's worth reminding ourselves what emergency and charity-based aid can and cannot do. Aid-supported scholarships have certainly helped send African girls to school (never mind that they won't be able to find a job in their own countries once they have graduated). This kind of aid can provide band-aid solutions to alleviate immediate suffering, but by its very nature cannot be the platform for long-term sustainable growth.

Whatever its strengths and weaknesses, such charity-based aid is relatively small beer when compared to the sea of money that floods Africa each year in government-to-government aid or aid from large development institutions such as the World Bank.

Over the past 60 years at least $1 trillion of development-related aid has been transferred from rich countries to Africa. Yet real per-capita income today is lower than it was in the 1970s, and more than 50% of the population—over 350 million people—live on less than a dollar a day, a figure that has nearly doubled in two decades.

Even after the very aggressive debt-relief campaigns in the 1990s, African countries still pay close to $20 billion in debt repayments per annum, a stark reminder that aid is not free. In order to keep the system going, debt is repaid at the expense of African education and health care. Well-meaning calls to cancel debt mean little when the cancellation is met with the fresh infusion of aid, and the vicious cycle starts up once again.

In 2005, just weeks ahead of a G8 conference that had Africa at the top of its agenda, the International Monetary Fund published a report entitled "Aid Will Not Lift Growth in Africa." The report cautioned that governments, donors and campaigners should be more modest in their claims that increased aid will solve Africa's problems. Despite such comments, no serious efforts have been made to wean Africa off this debilitating drug.

The most obvious criticism of aid is its links to rampant corruption. Aid flows destined to help the average African end up supporting bloated bureaucracies in the form of the poor-country governments and donor-funded non-governmental organizations. In a hearing before the U.S. Senate Committee on Foreign Relations in May 2004, Jeffrey Winters, a professor at Northwestern University, argued that the World Bank had participated in the corruption of roughly $100 billion of its loan funds intended for development.

As recently as 2002, the African Union, an organization of African nations, estimated that corruption was costing the continent $150 billion a year, as international donors were apparently turning a blind eye to the simple fact that aid money was inadvertently fueling graft. With few or no strings attached, it has been all too easy for the funds to be used for anything save the developmental purpose for which they were intended.

In Zaire—known today as the Democratic Republic of Congo—Irwin Blumenthal (whom the IMF had appointed to a post in the country's central bank) warned in 1978 that the system was so corrupt that there was "no (repeat, no) prospect for Zaire's creditors to get their money back." Still, the IMF soon gave the country the largest loan it had ever given an African nation. According to corruption watchdog agency Transparency International, Mobutu Sese Seko, Zaire's president from 1965 to 1997, is reputed to have stolen at least $5 billion from the country.

It's scarcely better today. A month ago, Malawi's former President Bakili Muluzi was charged with embezzling aid money worth $12 million. Zambia's former President Frederick Chiluba (a development darling during his 1991 to 2001 tenure) remains embroiled in a court case that has revealed millions of dollars frittered away from health, education and infrastructure toward his personal cash dispenser. Yet the aid keeps on coming.

A nascent economy needs a transparent and accountable government and an efficient civil service to help meet social needs. Its people need jobs and a belief in their country's future. A surfeit of aid has been shown to be unable to help achieve these goals.

A constant stream of "free" money is a perfect way to keep an inefficient or simply bad government in power. As aid flows in, there is nothing more for the government to do—it doesn't need to raise taxes, and as long as it pays the army, it doesn't have to take account of its disgruntled citizens. No matter that its citizens are disenfranchised (as with no taxation there can be no representation). All the government really needs to do is to court and cater to its foreign donors to stay in power.

Stuck in an aid world of no incentives, there is no reason for governments to seek other, better, more transparent ways of raising development finance (such as accessing the bond market, despite how hard that might be). The aid system encourages poor-country governments to pick up the phone and ask the donor agencies for the next capital infusion. It is no wonder that across Africa, over 70% of the public purse comes from foreign aid.

Bad Governments, Bad Debts

Perceived corruption in government is very high in Africa. African underdevelopment has [in 2006] become the focus of renewed major efforts to disburse more official aid and cancel overdue debts. It does not surprise that corruption-riddled governments of stagnating economies show little inclination to repay loans. The highly indebted, poor African countries—as well as Burma and Vietnam—invariably also display the worst corruption ratings. When outstanding loans from the World Bank and other official agencies are simply forgiven or serviced by the taxpayers of affluent countries, this creates 'moral hazard', the invitation to act irresponsibly. It also encourages both greater and more entrenched corruption and new borrowing to support the extravagant living standards of the elites. Such regimes also typically deny the citizens economic freedom.

Wolfgang Kasper,
Centre for Independent Studies Issue Analysis No. 67,
January 19, 2006.

In Ethiopia, where aid constitutes more than 90% of the government budget, a mere 2% of the country's population has access to mobile phones. (The African country average is around 30%.) Might it not be preferable for the government to earn money by selling its mobile phone license, thereby generating much-needed development income and also providing its citizens with telephone service that could, in turn, spur economic activity?

Look what has happened in Ghana, a country where after decades of military rule brought about by a coup, a pro-market government has yielded encouraging developments.

Farmers and fishermen now use mobile phones to communicate with their agents and customers across the country to find out where prices are most competitive. This translates into numerous opportunities for self-sustainability and income generation—which, with encouragement, could be easily replicated across the continent.

To advance a country's economic prospects, governments need efficient civil service. But civil service is naturally prone to bureaucracy, and there is always the incipient danger of self-serving cronyism and the desire to bind citizens in endless, time-consuming red tape. What aid does is to make that danger a grim reality. This helps to explain why doing business across much of Africa is a nightmare. In Cameroon, it takes a potential investor around 426 days to perform 15 procedures to gain a business license. What entrepreneur wants to spend 119 days filling out forms to start a business in Angola? He's much more likely to consider the U.S. (40 days and 19 procedures) or South Korea (17 days and 10 procedures).

Even what may appear as a benign intervention on the surface can have damning consequences. Say there is a mosquito-net maker in small-town Africa. Say he employs 10 people who together manufacture 500 nets a week. Typically, these 10 employees support upward of 15 relatives each. A Western government-inspired program generously supplies the affected region with 100,000 free mosquito nets. This promptly puts the mosquito net manufacturer out of business, and now his 10 employees can no longer support their 150 dependents. In a couple of years, most of the donated nets will be torn and useless, but now there is no mosquito net maker to go to. They'll have to get more aid. And African governments once again get to abdicate their responsibilities.

In a similar vein has been the approach to food aid, which historically has done little to support African farmers. Under the auspices of the U.S. Food for Peace program, each year millions of dollars are used to buy American-grown food that has to then be shipped across oceans. One wonders how a system of flooding foreign markets with American food, which puts local farmers out of business, actually helps better Africa. A better strategy would be to use aid money to buy food from farmers within the country, and then distribute that food to the local citizens in need.

Then there is the issue of "Dutch disease," a term that describes how large inflows of money can kill off a country's export sector, by driving up home prices and thus making their goods too expensive for export. Aid has the same effect. Large dollar-denominated aid windfalls that envelop fragile developing economies cause the domestic currency to strengthen against foreign currencies. This is catastrophic for jobs in the poor country where people's livelihoods depend on being relatively competitive in the global market.

To fight aid-induced inflation, countries have to issue bonds to soak up the subsequent glut of money swamping the economy. In 2005, for example, Uganda was forced to issue such bonds to mop up excess liquidity to the tune of $700 million. The interest payments alone on this were a staggering $110 million, to be paid annually.

The stigma associated with countries relying on aid should also not be underestimated or ignored. It is the rare investor that wants to risk money in a country that is unable to stand on its own feet and manage its own affairs in a sustainable way.

Africa remains the most unstable continent in the world, beset by civil strife and war. Since 1996, 11 countries have been embroiled in civil wars. According to the Stockholm International Peace Research Institute, in the 1990s, Africa had more wars than the rest of the world combined. Although my country, Zambia, has not had the unfortunate experience of an outright civil war, growing up I experienced first-hand the discomfort of living under curfew (where everyone had to be in their homes between 6 P.M. and 6 A.M., which meant racing from work and school) and faced the fear of the uncertain outcomes of an attempted coup in 1991—sadly, experiences not uncommon to many Africans.

Civil clashes are often motivated by the knowledge that by seizing the seat of power, the victor gains virtually unfettered access to the package of aid that comes with it. In the last few months alone, there have been at least three political upheavals across the continent, in Mauritania, Guinea and Guinea Bissau (each of which remains reliant on foreign aid). Madagascar's government was just overthrown in a coup this past week. The ongoing political volatility across the continent serves as a reminder that aid-financed efforts to force-feed democracy to economies facing ever-growing poverty and difficult economic prospects remain, at best, precariously vulnerable. Long-term political success can only be achieved once a solid economic trajectory has been established.

Proponents of aid are quick to argue that the $13 billion ($100 billion in today's terms) aid of the post–World War II Marshall Plan helped pull back a broken Europe from the brink of an economic abyss, and that aid could work, and would work, if Africa had a good policy environment.

The aid advocates skirt over the point that the Marshall Plan interventions were short, sharp and finite, unlike the open-ended commitments which imbue governments with a sense of entitlement rather than encouraging innovation. And aid supporters spend little time addressing the mystery of why a country in good working order would seek aid rather than other, better forms of financing. No country has ever achieved economic success by depending on aid to the degree that many African countries do.

The good news is we know what works; what delivers growth and reduces poverty. We know that economies that rely on open-ended commitments of aid almost universally fail, and those that do not depend on aid succeed. The latter is true for economically successful countries such as China and

India, and even closer to home, in South Africa and Botswana. Their strategy of development finance emphasizes the important role of entrepreneurship and markets over a staid aid-system of development that preaches hand-outs.

African countries could start by issuing bonds to raise cash. To be sure, the traditional capital markets of the U.S. and Europe remain challenging. However, African countries could explore opportunities to raise capital in more non-traditional markets such as the Middle East and China (whose foreign exchange reserves are more than $4 trillion). Moreover, the current market malaise provides an opening for African countries to focus on acquiring credit ratings (a prerequisite to accessing the bond markets), and preparing themselves for the time when the capital markets return to some semblance of normalcy.

Governments need to attract more foreign direct investment by creating attractive tax structures and reducing the red tape and complex regulations for businesses. African nations should also focus on increasing trade; China is one promising partner. And Western countries can help by cutting off the cycle of giving something for nothing. It's time for a change.

"GM technology offers the hope of doubled crop yields per hectare of arable land. A hungry world needs such research."

Genetically Modified Crops Can Help Ease World Hunger

Gustav Nossal

Victoria, one of the most populous states in Australia, placed a moratorium on growing genetically modified (GM) crops in 2003. Gustav Nossal, a highly respected research biologist whose work has led to a knighthood and many other awards, chaired the panel that lifted this moratorium in 2008. In the following viewpoint, Nossal explains the arguments he heard for and against lifting the ban. He then goes on to claim that GM foods are necessary to reduce hunger, especially in the Third World. He believes that proof of adequate testing will likely persuade the people of that Australian state that GM foods are safe and as beneficial as genetically modified drugs.

As you read, consider the following questions:

1. What are some of the GM crops that Nossal says current research in Australia is directed toward?

Gustav Nossal, "GM Food Can Help Ease Hunger," *The Age*, June 23, 2008. Reproduced by permission of the author.

2. What concern does the author have with the irradiation of crops to speed mutation?

3. What nutrition deficiencies does Nossal claim are rampant in the Third World?

Chairing the [Australian state of Victoria's government] review of the moratorium on genetically modified [GM] canola [a hybridized vegetable oil crop] proved a challenging task. It was also a heartening exercise in democracy at work. The panel received 248 substantive submissions from the public as well as 1177 that were essentially form letters. Further, 36 groups were invited to meet the panel to discuss their views.

Reasons to Stop GM Production

Those who wished the moratorium to continue gave essentially five groups of reasons:

- Genetic engineering is somehow against nature or God's plan.

- GM foods might pose health or environmental risks, hazards that had not been properly investigated.

- GM foods gave too much power to a small group of multinational corporations.

- Growth of GMOs [genetically modified organisms] might imperil Australia's clean, green image by, for example, damaging the business of organic farmers.

- Farmers might be forgoing a price premium that GM canola could command in export markets.

Reasons to Approve GM Production

Those who argued for a suspension of the moratorium reasoned along four lines.

Top Eight GM Countries

No.	Country	2007 hectares (million)	2008 hectares (million)	GM crops
1	United States of America	57.7	62.5	Alfalfa, canola, cotton, corn, soybean, squash, sugar beet, papaya
2	Argentina	19.1	21.0	Cotton, corn, soybean
3	Brazil	15.0	15.8	Cotton, corn, soybean
4	India	6.2	7.6	Cotton
5	Canada	7.0	7.6	Canola, corn, soybean, sugar beet
6	China	3.8	3.8	Cotton, papaya, petunia, poplar, sweet pepper, tomato
7	Paraguay	2.6	2.7	Soybean
8	South Africa	1.8	1.8	Cotton, corn, soybean

TAKEN FROM: Monsanto (Australia), "GM Crops: Thirteen Million Farmers and Thirteen Successful Years of Commercialisation," February 13, 2009. www. monsanto.com.au

- They wanted growers to have choice. In fact, 29 organisations participating in the grain supply chain signed a Single Vision Statement favouring the marketing of both GM and non-GM canola, so that those growers who wished to take advantage of the yield improvements and of the environmental benefits of the biodegradable herbicides used with GM canola (rather than the toxic, non-biodegradable triazines for conventional canola) could do so.

- The industry was convinced it had the capacity to maintain segregation of GM from non-GM grain right across the supply chain.

- The financial benefits to Victoria were seen as $170–$180 million to 2016, and $29 million a year thereafter.

- Submissions argued forcefully about the downstream effects of continuing the moratorium.

A rejection of the GM approach would imperil research on many new traits more exciting than glyphosate or glufosinate resistance.

To mention just a few, current research is directed towards drought-resistant wheat, virus-resistant white clover, allergen-free rye grass, frost-resistant horticultural products and bananas resistant to soil pests.

Furthermore, banning the industry's most powerful research tool was seen as having a devastating effect on corporate investment and a demoralising influence on prospective agriculture students and their teachers. One university authority claimed that five more years of moratorium would effectively destroy agricultural innovation in Victoria.

A Decision Is Made

After six months of meetings, extensive reading, interviewing of experts and robust discussion, our panel was unanimous in recommending a lifting of the moratorium. We urged that the market should be allowed to work, that growers should be given choice, that industry self-regulation was to be encouraged and that the Government should work with the organics sector to identify barriers to and opportunities for growth.

It is worthwhile remembering that GM methods of improving agricultural traits build on about 6000 years of conventional plant breeding to improve food crops. It substitutes high-tech ways of introducing desirable traits for the Darwinian process of random mutation and selection.

One slightly amusing aspect is that in conventional plant breeding programs, the process of mutation is often speeded up by irradiation. If there are fears of unwanted, unpredicted and undesirable side effects, how much more would these be apparent in the totally random process of mutation that irradiation accelerates?

Critics of GM foods often forget that between the first insertion of some new, desirable trait and the commercial release of the relevant GM crop, there is a process of at least a decade of applied research and development. This is precisely because it is important to remove the risk of some unpredicted undesirable trait in the plant involved. The quickest way for the much-maligned multinational to go broke would be to release a plant variety that did harm instead of good.

GM Drugs Once Controversial

The present debate about GM foods is like that about GM pharmaceuticals in the 1980s. At that time, fears of GM ran so high that, at one stage, the mayor of Cambridge, Massachusetts, threatened to shut down all the laboratories of Harvard University that were conducting genetic engineering research.

Who now worries about the pharmaceuticals that resulted from GM processes: interferons to fight virus infections, some cancers and multiple sclerosis; the hugely effective vaccines against hepatitis B and the human papillomavirus—the first anti-cancer vaccines in history; erythropoietin to revolutionise quality of life in the chronic kidney disease patient; G-CSF, the unique Australian invention to help restore the white cell count after cancer chemotherapy or bone marrow transplantation?

All the merchants of doom about GM pharmaceuticals have long since been silenced. Thus it will be with GM foods.

My chief reason for engaging in this debate concerns the Third World. While there is little calorie malnutrition except in areas of disaster or conflict, there is still malnutrition in quality of food. This involves content of protein and essential amino acids as well as micronutrients such as vitamin A, iron and iodine. GM technology offers the hope of devising staple crops richer in these essential constituents. Ought we to constrain the research that brings these about? The Bill and Melinda Gates Foundation [a philanthropic organization founded by Microsoft entrepreneur Bill Gates and his wife], for one, thinks not. And Monsanto [a multinational firm] believes that GM technology offers the hope of doubled crop yields per hectare of arable land. A hungry world needs such research.

> "People go hungry because they're either poor, powerless, both, or have no land to grow food on. GM crops don't change this."

Genetically Modified Food Will Not Ease World Hunger

Andrew Simms

Andrew Simms is the policy director of the New Economics Foundation and author of Ecological Debt: The Health of the Planet and the Wealth of Nations. *In the following viewpoint, he argues that genetically modified (GM) foods are being sold to the world through biased scientific reports and pro-biotech industry politicking. Simms contends that many developing nations object to GM foods to feed their poor populations, claiming that these foods are not environmentally friendly or proven safe for consumption. Simms believes that sustainable agriculture is a better solution to global hunger.*

As you read, consider the following questions:

1. What argument does Simms say is a form of "moral blackmail" used by GM food promoters?

2. What does the author say creates "a massive market distortion in the global food system in favour of multinational companies"?

3. According to Simms, why does the world hear only one side of the GM debate—the side of the big biotech corporations?

The sound of one hand clapping should greet the behaviour of "rational" scientists, businessmen and politicians in the debate on the future of genetically modified [GM] food.

One member of the government's review panel resigned because of its "naive" and unbalanced approach. Another formally complained that he was threatened with the loss of research funding if he was critical of GM technology. In the most staggering example of a conflict of interest in recent times, a Monsanto [a GM food promoter] employee was reportedly commissioned to write the first draft of the panel's report concerning GM safety issues.

Scientists Show Their Bias

Icing on this less than rational cake was added by David King, chairman of the panel and chief government scientific adviser, who used the experience of the US to reassure the public. GM food has been eaten there since around 1996 with no obvious adverse effects. But absence of evidence of harm is not evidence of the absence of harm.

What emerges is an automatic cultural bias in the scientific community towards invasive, hi-tech solutions to complex social, environmental and economic problems. Regardless of whether or not they are best—or even appropriate.

Because why, after all, do we need GM crops? Even if the world was short of food, which it is not, available evidence suggests that using what is called "sustainable agriculture"—a mixture of environmental and pro-poor approaches to growing food—brings massively higher increases in overall productivity than anything achieved through genetic modification.

Consumers and supermarkets do not want them. Only a hard core of biotech businesses, researchers and their political allies are bothered.

Feeding the Poor Is a Poor Excuse

Floundering for winning arguments, they've settled on a kind of moral blackmail, the modern equivalent of patriotism being the last resort of the scoundrel. We should commercially introduce GM crops, they say, because we need to feed the poor.

When this argument was first used aggressively by Monsanto in the late 1990s, the poor had other ideas. African delegates from Ethiopia to Burundi, Senegal and Mozambique, at special negotiations of the UN Food and Agriculture Organisation [FAO] "strongly" objected that "the image of the poor and hungry from our countries is being used by giant multinational corporations to push a technology that is neither safe, environmentally friendly, nor economically beneficial to us".

They were convinced that the "feed the world" argument was a huge (genetically modified) red herring. Since then, the GM lobbyists just shout louder. [U.S. president] George Bush accused the European Union of starving hungry people because of its caution over GM crops.

Obscuring the Real Problems

Why are the new scoundrels so wrong? The arguments need repetition. People go hungry because they're either poor, powerless, both, or have no land to grow food on. GM crops don't change this. Britain's experience has been enormously problematic. The poor, majority world has no chance to regulate, monitor or segregate GM crops.

Profits over People

Monsanto and other biotech companies continue to exercise extraordinary influence over governments and their regulatory apparatuses, ushering poorly tested and potentially hazardous products through weak approval processes. Bribery has been used as a tool to overcome environmental risk assessment hurdles, and unethical and immoral media campaigns have been waged. These are all troubling developments that bespeak a profound disconnection between the profit-driven goals of agribusiness and the clear desires of citizens around the world for healthy, sustainable food systems.

Carmen Améndola et al.,
Friends of the Earth International, January 2006.

Almost everything scientists are trying to achieve by genetically modifying crops can be achieved in other, less risky ways. Whether the problem is pest or weed control, drought tolerance, yield or nutrition, there are countless, though poorly supported, farming methods that can be used before needing to open pandora's box of genetic tricks. GM advocates seem only to have discovered the cause of poverty eradication now that they have something to sell.

Increasingly restrictive global intellectual property laws, which are a precondition for commercial GM crop technology, further weaken the bargaining power of the poor and hungry. They create a massive market distortion in the global food system in favour of multinational companies that already enjoy near-monopoly positions. Most worrying, according to aid agencies, is that the GM lobby is almost entirely ignorant about how and why people actually go hungry, and how to change it.

Big Corporations Are Wrong

Nature has no advertising budget. Advocates of sustainable agriculture also tend to be poor and marginalised. The biotech firms, on the other hand, have armies of PR [public relations] and sales people, researchers, lawyers and lobbyists. They fear that there should be a proper comparative assessment of the relative merits of GM, conventional farming, and sustainable and organic agriculture, which would most likely show that a mixture of efficient public distribution systems, sustainable agriculture, land reform, education and guaranteed basic healthcare would make GM crops at best a rare, final resort, and more often completely irrelevant.

This is an old cycle repeated. Huge hype around a hi-tech magic bullet swiftly followed by brutal logistical, technical and economic reality.

Remember vitamin A–enriched rice, meant to help prevent blindness in malnourished people? It seemed like such a good idea until it emerged that you had to eat a truckload to get the required dose [of Vitamin A]. As Franz Simmersbach of the FAO said: "Its as if vitamin A research makes researchers go blind!"

Magic is fine when you read *Harry Potter*, but not when you live in the real world.

Periodical Bibliography

The following articles have been selected to supplement the diverse views presented in this chapter.

Bill Freese — "Biotech Snake Oil," *Multinational Monitor*, September/October 2008.

Duncan Green — "Power v. Poverty," *New Statesman*, June 23, 2008.

Stuart L. Hart — "Converging on Green," *BizEd*, July/August 2009.

Samuel Loewenberg — "Global Food Crisis Looks Set to Continue," *Lancet*, October 4, 2008.

Debora Mackenzie — "Rich Countries Grab Farmland from Poorer Ones," *New Scientist*, December 6, 2008.

Nancy A. Naples — "Crossing Borders: Community Activism, Globalization, and Social Justice," *Social Problems*, February 2009.

Mary Anastasia O'Grady — "Aid Keeps Latin America Poor," *Wall Street Journal*, April 6, 2009.

J. Timmons Roberts et al. — "Has Foreign Aid Been Greened?" *Environment*, January 2009.

Peter Singer — "America's Shame," *Chronicle of Higher Education*, March 13, 2009.

Roger D. Stone — "Water Wisdom," *American Prospect*, June 2008.

For Further Discussion

Chapter 1

1. Brad Schiller maintains that the supposed income gap is an exaggeration because it does not account for the fact that a large pool of low-income immigrants is weighting the bottom end of the spectrum. Oriando Ibarra, on the other hand, argues that the salaries of the wealthiest Americans are weighting the top end of the spectrum. Whose analysis do you find more convincing? Explain, using evidence from the viewpoints.

2. After reading the viewpoints by Chuck Norris and Steve Crawley, explain whether you think a Fair Tax system—one that taxes only consumption—would be a more equitable and just form of taxation. When composing your answer, be sure to include your views on Fair Tax advocates' claims that an income tax is unconstitutional.

3. James Sherk makes the argument that raising the national minimum wage will not help reduce poverty in America. Analyze Sherk's claims and explain how you would respond to each of them. You may use evidence from Holly Sklar's viewpoint and from outside sources to bolster your assertions.

Chapter 2

1. Review the viewpoints by Ari Melber and Gary Becker; then explain your own feelings about affirmative action policies. Do you believe they are needed to promote equal opportunity in education and job placement? Or are these programs outdated? How far do you think America has come in providing equal opportunity for all citizens regardless of race, ethnicity, or gender? Use arguments from the viewpoints to support your answers.

2. Chris Dodd believes that gay marriage should be legal in the United States, a nation that, he asserts, has progressed enough in the realm of social justice to recognize that bigotry of this sort cannot be tolerated. David Blankenhorn counters that gay marriage hurts by dismissing traditional notions of marriage and depriving children of their birthright if they happen to become adopted by a gay couple. Do you agree with Blankenhorn that marriage is an institution designed to further procreation, or is it merely a symbol of commitment and love between adults, as Dodd contends? Explain why you favor one opinion over the other.

3. As the arguments of three of the authors in this chapter illustrate, the notion of restitution for slavery and the treatment of Native Americans rests on the fact that today's generation can be held liable for the sins of the past. Using evidence from the arguments of Clarence Lang, Joe Schriner, and Michael Reagan, decide whether you agree that financial compensation or the return of land by modern society can atone for ill treatment of ancestors a hundred or more years ago. In your answer, also contend with the fact that arguably similar reparations were paid to Holocaust victims by the West German government and Swiss banks.

Chapter 3

1. The first two viewpoints in Chapter 3 address disparities in wages earned by men and women. Ashley English and Ariane Hegewisch contend that the gender wage gap is a very real problem that creates hardship for women and families. Stephen Jarosek, on the other hand, argues that the gender wage gap does not exist and is a construct of feminists. Further, he believes that focus on the wage gap and policies put in place to decrease the gap have had an overall negative impact on men. Review the two view-

points and decide which one you find more convincing. Use quotes from the viewpoints to support your answer.

2. While the 2008 presidential election saw a Democratic woman in close contention for the presidential nomination and the Republican Party nominate a woman as a vice presidential candidate, debate has continued as to whether the political glass ceiling has been broken. Much concern revolves around the media portrayal and public scrutiny of these two women. Review the two viewpoints by Marie Cocco and Michelle D. Bernard, and read some additional articles written during the primary and presidential campaigns. Do you think that the women candidates faced more severe judgment than male candidates would? Was sexist language used when describing these two candidates, or were they treated the same as the male candidates? Use specific examples from the coverage you find to support your claims.

Chapter 4

1. Alexander Downer and Binoy Barman hold different perceptions of the impact of globalization on developing nations. Downer believes that free trade has improved living standards and given citizens in developing nations choices and opportunities they would not otherwise have. Barman contends that globalization forces Western views and economic practices on developing nations, depriving them of choice. What rhetorical strategies does each author use to make his argument? Whose argument do you believe and why? In answering the latter part of the question, explain whether the author's evidence and rhetorical strategy had anything to do with your agreement with his position.

2. In her viewpoint, Dambisa Moyo claims that foreign aid money—while well intentioned—often is appropriated by autocratic governments and thus never provides a tangible benefit to the citizens of developing nations. Additionally,

she argues that nonmonetary financial aid—such as goods and foodstuffs—is potentially threatening to burgeoning markets in developing nations. Read more on the subject of foreign aid and the notion of accountability and explain how you think foreign aid might better be distributed so that its impact will be felt by those who most need it.

3. Andrew Simms condemns genetically modified (GM) food promoters, saying "they've settled on a kind of moral blackmail, the modern equivalent of patriotism being the last resort of the scoundrel. We should commercially introduce GM crops, they say, because we need to feed the poor." After reading Simms's viewpoint and that of Gustav Nossal, explain whether you agree with Simms's claim. Is the overriding need to feed the world's poor enough of an argument to advocate genetically modified foods as a solution? Use evidence from the viewpoints to support your answer.

Organizations to Contact

The editors have compiled the following list of organizations concerned with the issues debated in this book. The descriptions are derived from materials provided by the organizations. All have publications or information available for interested readers. The list was compiled on the date of publication of the present volume; the information provided here may change. Be aware that many organizations take several weeks or longer to respond to inquiries, so allow as much time as possible.

American Civil Liberties Union (ACLU)

125 Broad St., 18th Floor, New York, NY   10004
(212) 607-3300 • fax: (212) 607-3318
Web site: www.aclu.org

The ACLU works to ensure that the civil rights of all Americans are observed and upheld. They provide legal counsel to individuals whose civil rights—right to free speech, equal protection, due process, and right to privacy—have been violated in order to make certain that these rights are not infringed on in the future. Often the ACLU's aid is provided to individuals whose rights are commonly ignored, such as ethnic and racial minorities, women, lesbians, gay men, bisexuals, and transgendered people. Information about current social justice projects being conducted by the organization can be found on its Web site along with briefing papers about the importance of human rights and equality for all people.

American Enterprise Institute (AEI)

1150 Seventeenth St. NW, Washington, DC   20036
(202) 862-5800 • fax: (202) 862-7177
Web site: www.aei.org

AEI is a nonpartisan public-policy institute dedicated to analyzing the impact of government policies on the American people, publishing the findings at conferences and in policy reports, and providing suggestions to policy makers about the best course of action in the future. The institute has examined many issues of social justice, including affirmative action, race and gender, tax policy, and international aid. Reports on these topics and others can be read on the AEI Web site. Additional articles addressing social justice issues can be found in the bimonthly publication of the institute, the *American*.

Americans for Fair Taxation

PO Box 27487, Houston, TX   77227-7487
(713) 963-9023 • fax: (713) 963-8403
e-mail: info@fairtax.org
Web site: www.fairtax.org

Americans for Fair Taxation advocates for the implementation of the FairTax plan, which would abolish the Internal Revenue Service along with all current income taxes and institute a national, federal sales tax. Thus, workers would receive their full paycheck with no tax deductions and all tax revenues would be generated by the purchase of goods, making the tax system fair and transparent, according to the organization. The Fair-Tax Web site provides comprehensive research papers assessing the impact of a fair tax system on areas such as agriculture, business, real estate, charity, and a range of demographics.

Amnesty International

5 Penn Plaza, 16th Floor, New York, NY   10001
(212) 807-8400 • fax: (212) 463-9193
e-mail: admin-us@aiusa.org
Web site: www.amnesty.org

Amnesty International is a global human rights organization that seeks to ensure that human rights are guaranteed to individuals worldwide. With international offices in more than eighty countries, Amnesty conducts work to ensure social justice on the local level with assistance from global partners. The organization's work focuses on human rights within specific areas such as business, discrimination, poverty, and sexual orientation and gender identity. Information about current campaigns and activities can be accessed on the Amnesty International Web site.

Cato Institute

1000 Massachusetts Ave. NW, Washington, DC 20001-5403
(202) 842-0200 • fax: (202) 842-3490
Web site: www.cato.org

The Cato Institute, a libertarian public policy organization, constructs its views utilizing the ideals of limited government, individual liberty, free-market economics, and peace. Issues relating to social justice are addressed within a wide variety of topics covered by Cato, including law and civil liberties, international economics and development, education and child policy, and tax and budget policy. Cato publications include the tri-annual *Cato Journal*, the quarterly *Cato's Letters*, and the bimonthly *Cato Policy Report*.

Global Policy Forum (GPF)

777 UN Plaza, Suite 3D, New York, NY 10017
(212) 557-3161 • fax: (212) 557-3165
e-mail: gpf@globalpolicy.org
Web site: www.globalpolicy.org

GPF acts as a watchdog over the United Nations to ensure accountability and citizen participation in the implementation of international policies. The organization conducts extensive research on a variety of topics, including globalization, international justice, and social and economic policy. The findings are published in reports and further proliferated through media interviews and conferences. The GPF seeks to ensure that social justice and equality are promoted and maintained in the actions of the UN. The GPF Web site provides access to forum reports and commentary.

The Heritage Foundation

214 Massachusetts Ave. NE, Washington, DC 20002-4999
(202) 546-4400 • fax: (202) 546-8328

e-mail: info@heritage.org
Web site: www.heritage.org

The Heritage Foundation promotes the conservative principles of free enterprise, limited government, individual freedom, traditional American values, and a strong national defense. The foundation has held conferences such as The First International Conservative Conference on Social Justice, and Social Justice Is Not What You Think It Is, inquiring into the nature of social justice and the action that must be taken to promote it. Additionally, the topic of social justice has been covered in Heritage's research into individual topics such as economics, education, family and marriage, welfare, and foreign aid. The Heritage Foundation *Backgrounder* series provides general information about these topics, and individual scholars' commentary can be accessed and read on the Heritage Web site.

Independent Women's Forum (IWF)
4400 Jenifer St., Suite 240, Washington, DC   20015
(202) 419-1820 • fax: (202) 419-1821
e-mail: info@iwf.org
Web site: www.iwf.org

The IWF examines issues relating to women, men, and families and promotes conservative principles such as limited government, legal equality, property rights, free markets, traditional family values, and a strong national defense. The organization focuses on both domestic and international issues, including women's studies, feminism, human and women's rights, and economics. Generally, IWF scholars believe that women are experiencing greater equality now than at any other point in history and that many policies implemented to address perceived inequalities are not necessary. Policy papers addressing social justice issues, such as "Proportionality Is Not What High Schools Need," and "Excellence, Not Gender Parity, Should Be Priority for STEM Faculty," can be read online.

National Organization for Women (NOW)

1100 H St. NW, 3rd Floor, Washington, DC   20005
(202) 628-8669 • fax: (202) 785-8576
e-mail: www.now.org
Web site: www.now.org

NOW is a national organization of feminist activists seeking to end discrimination, sexism, racism, and homophobia; ensure reproductive rights for women; put a stop to violence against women; and advocate for social justice and equality in American society. With regard to each topic, the organization provides background information as well as current news about the issue and ways that individuals can take action to make a change. Copies of reports concerning social justice issues can be read on NOW's Web site.

United Nations (UN)

140 E. Forty-fifth St., New York, NY   10017
(212) 415-4000 • fax: (212) 415-4443
e-mail: usa@un.int
Web site: www.un.org

Founded in 1945 following World War II, the UN is an international organization of member countries seeking to maintain international peace and security, foster friendly relations among countries, and promote social progress, improved living standards, and human rights. Much of the UN's work focuses on peacekeeping and peacebuilding; however, individual committees are committed to specific tasks to improve human life worldwide. Committees concerned with social justice issues include the UN Commission on Human Rights and the UN Development Program. Each works on specific areas— human rights and development in these cases—to address inequality and help create programs to combat social injustice. The UN Web site provides links to these specific commissions' Web sites as well as reports on the current state of social justice issues worldwide.

Urban Institute
2100 M St. NW, Washington, DC   20037
(202) 833-7200
Web site: www.urban.org

Founded in 1968, the Urban Institute has been working for over forty years to analyze and evaluate policies' effectiveness in fostering economic growth and prosperity in American cities. Topics addressed by the institute include economy and taxes, employment, international issues, and race, ethnicity and gender. The institute examines each of these issues in detail and assesses income disparities, discrimination, human rights observance abroad, and commitment to social justice. Reports and commentaries by institute scholars can be read online.

U.S. Agency for International Development (USAID)
Information Center, Ronald Reagan Bldg.
Washington, DC   20523-1000
(202) 712-4810 • fax: (202) 216-3524
Web site: www.usaid.gov

USAID was created in 1961 to act as the federal agency in charge of providing federal assistance to countries around the world. The office was created for two purposes—to promote American policy interests globally and to aid those in developing countries in creating better lives for themselves. Specifically, USAID seeks to foster economic growth, agriculture and trade, global health, and democracy. Information about current USAID policies and programs can be read on the agency's Web site.

World Socialist Web Site
Socialist Equality Party, Oak Park, MI   48237
Web site: www.wsws.org

Published by the International Committee of the Fourth International—the leadership body of the world socialist movement—the World Socialist Web site provides information about socialism and its benefits to the United States and the world. Commentary is presented about inequality in America, workers struggles, and the world economy among other topics. The World Socialist Web site opposes capitalism, which is identified as the cause of social inequality worldwide, and seeks to unite the working class so that they can create social change and justice on an international level. Information about socialist ideas and policies can be read on the Web site.

Bibliography of Books

Robert M. Baird and Stuart E. Rosenbaum — *Same-Sex Marriage: The Moral and Legal Debate*. Amherst, NY: Prometheus, 2004.

Larry M. Bartels — *Unequal Democracy: The Political Economy of the New Gilded Age*. New York: Russell Sage Foundation, 2008.

Brian Berry — *Why Social Justice Matters*. Cambridge: Polity, 2005.

Mary Frances Berry — *My Face Is Black Is True: Callie House and the Struggle for Ex-slave Reparations*. New York: Knopf, 2005.

Gillian Brock — *Global Justice: A Cosmopolitan Account*. New York: Oxford University Press, 2009.

Darrell Cleveland, ed. — *When "Minorities Are Strongly Encouraged to Apply": Diversity and Affirmative Action in Higher Education*. New York: Peter Lang, 2009.

Alice Hendrickson Eagly — *Through the Labyrinth: The Truth About How Women Become Leaders*. Boston: Harvard Business School Press, 2007.

William A. Easterly — *Reinventing Foreign Aid*. Cambridge, MA: MIT Press, 2008.

Bill Fletcher, Jr.   *Solidarity Divided: The Crisis in Organized Labor and a New Path Toward Social Justice.* Berkeley and Los Angeles: University of California Press, 2008.

James R. Flynn   *Where Have All the Minorities Gone? Race, Class, and Ideals in America.* New York: Cambridge University Press, 2008.

Gavin Fridell   *Fair Trade Coffee: The Prospects and Pitfalls of Market-Driven Social Justice.* Toronto: University of Toronto Press, 2007.

Michael J. Graetz   *100 Million Unnecessary Returns: A Simple, Fair, and Competitive Tax Plan for the United States.* New Haven, CT: Yale University Press, 2008.

David B. Grusky and Szonja Szelényi   *The Inequality Reader: Contemporary and Foundational Readings in Race, Class, and Gender.* Boulder, CO: Westview, 2007.

Chester Hartman   *Challenges to Equality: Poverty and Race in America.* Armonk, NY: M.E. Sharpe, 2001.

Charles P. Henry   *Long Overdue: The Politics of Racial Reparations.* New York: New York University Press, 2007.

David Horowitz   *Uncivil Wars: The Controversy over Reparations for Slavery.* San Francisco: Encounter, 2002.

Edward J.
McCaffery

Fair Not Flat: How to Make the Tax System Better and Simpler. Chicago: University of Chicago Press, 2002.

Louis A. Picard
and Terry F. Buss

A Fragile Balance: Re-examining the History of Foreign Aid, Security, and Diplomacy. Sterling, VA: Kumarian, 2009.

Jonathan Rauch

Gay Marriage: Why It Is Good for Gays, Good for Straights, and Good for America. New York: Holt, 2004.

Stan Ringen

What Democracy Is For: On Freedom and Moral Government. Princeton, NJ: Princeton University Press, 2007.

Chloe Schwenke

Reclaiming Value in International Development: The Moral Dimensions of Development Policy and Practice in Poor Countries. Westport, CT: Praeger, 2009.

Peter Singer

The Life You Can Save: Acting Now to End World Poverty. New York: Random House, 2009.

Glenn T. Stanton
and Bill Maier

Marriage on Trial: The Case Against Same-Sex Marriage and Parenting. Downers Grove, IL: InterVarsity Press, 2004.

Andrew Sullivan

Same-Sex Marriage, Pro and Con: A Reader. New York: Vintage, 2004.

Mary Ann
Tétreault and
Ronnie D.
Lipschutz

Global Politics as if People Mattered. Lanham, MD: Rowman & Littlefield, 2009.

Sue Thomas and Clyde Wilcox, eds.	*Women and Elective Office: Past, Present, and Future.* New York: Oxford University Press, 2005.
Sue Tolleson-Rinehart and Jyl J. Johnson, eds.	*Gender and American Politics: Women, Men, and the Political Process.* Armonk, NY: M.E. Sharpe, 2005.
Jerold L. Waltman	*The Case for the Living Wage.* New York: Algora, 2004.

Index

F

G

Social Justice

women's political advance-
ment and, 148
United States (U.S.)
Census Bureau, 29, 30, 31, 33,
104, 137
Department of Justice (DOJ),
142
Food for Peace program, 186–
187
Labor Department, 23, 33
as meritocracy, 77–78
PATRIOT Act, 95
poverty rate in, 56, 58
Senate Committee on Foreign
Relations, 183
technology catch-up in, 158
Treasury Department, 45

V

Value Added Tax (VAT), 44
Vargas, Elizabeth, 152
Vedder, Richard, 55–56
Voting Rights Act, 96

W

Wage stagnation, 25, 30
See also Gender wage gap
Wall Street Journal (newspaper),
119
War on Drugs, 95
Wascher, William, 56, 57
Washington Post (newspaper), 120,
142
Water rights, 16
Wealth disparity
demographics of, 15–16
income gap and, 20–21

minimum wage and, 49–50
Welfare system
antipathy to, 96
for children, 100
de facto national, 43–44
international, 17
White Earth Land Preservation
Project, 108–109
The White Man's Burden
(Easterly), 176
Winters, Jeffrey, 183
Wolff, Edward N., 15
Women's issues. See Gender wage
gap; Glass ceiling concerns
Worker exploitation, 23–24
Working mothers, 137, 139
World Bank, 157, 160, 163, 182,
183, 185
World Conference Against Racism,
101
World Health Organization
(WHO), 176
World Institute for Development
Economics Research, 15
World Trade Organization
(WTO), 170
World Water Forum, 16

Y

Youth wage gap, 126

Z

Zaire, 183–184
Zambia, 184, 187
Zimbabwe, 164
Zinn, Howard, 106

226